The
VINTAGE
BAKER

The
VINTAGE
BAKER

MORE THAN 50 RECIPES

from Butterscotch Pecan Curls to Sour Cream Jumbles

JESSIE SHEEHAN

Photographs by **ALICE GAO**

CHRONICLE BOOKS

SAN FRANCISCO

DEDICATION

To my grandmother, Hyla: Whose lemon velvet sheet cake is one for the history books. And to my parents: For always filling the pantry with Nabisco Double Stuf Oreos and Drake's Devil Dogs. My sweet tooth would be nowhere without you.

Library of Congress Cataloging-in-Publication Data
Names: Sheehan, Jessie, author. | Gao, Alice, photographer.
Title: The vintage baker: more than 50 recipes from butterscotch pecan curls to sour cream jumbles / by Jessie Sheehan ; photographs by Alice Gao. Description: San Francisco : Chronicle Books, [2018]
Identifiers: LCCN 2017024415 | ISBN 9781452163871 (hc : alk. paper)
Subjects: LCSH: Baking. | Desserts. | LCGFT: Cookbooks. Classification:
LCC TX763 .S4257 2018 | DDC 641.81/5–dc23 LC record available at https://lccn.loc.gov/2017024415

Manufactured in China

MIX
Paper from responsible sources
FSC™ C008047

Photographs by **Alice Gao**   Designed by **Lizzie Vaughan**
Prop styling by **Kira Corbin**   Typesetting by **Howie Severson**
Food styling by **Diana Yen**   Typeset in Baskerville, Gotham, and Lulo Clean

Interior line art inspired by the *Bond Bread Cookbook*, General Baking Company, 1933.
Vintage interior art, Courtesy of Kraft Heinz Foods Company.
Double Stuf Oreos are a registered trademark of Intercontinental Great Brands LLC.
Drake's Devil Dogs and Yodels are registered trademarks of McKee Foods.
Kellogg's Rice Krispies and Pop Tarts are registered trademarks of Kellogg NA Co.
Kix Cereal and Pillsbury Bake-Off are registered trademarks of General Mills.
Red Hots are a registered trademark of Ferrara USA.

10 9 8 7 6 5 4 3 2

Chronicle Books LLC
680 Second Street
San Francisco, California 94107
www.chroniclebooks.com

CONTENTS

LET'S HAVE A PARTY

Banana Fritters

1 cup flour
2 teaspoons baking powder
¼ teaspoon salt

¼ cup milk
1 tablespoon lemon juice
1 egg
3 bananas

Mix and sift dry ingredients. Add beaten others in order. Force bananas through sieve before adding. Beat thoroughly. Drop by spoonfuls into hot fat. Drain and sprinkle with powdered sugar.

Cinnamon Buns

2¼ cups flour
1 teaspoon salt
4 teaspoons baking powder
2 tablespoons shortening
1 egg

½ cup water
½ cup sugar
2 teaspoons cinnamon
4 tablespoons seedless raisins

Sift 2 tablespoons of measured sugar with flour, salt and baking powder; rub shortening in lightly; add beaten egg to water and add slowly. Roll out ¼ inch thick on floured board; brush with melted butter, sprinkle with sugar, cinnamon, and raisins. Roll as for jelly roll; cut into 1½-inch pieces; place with cut edges up on greased pan, sprinkle with sugar and cinnamon. Bake in moderate oven 30 to 35 minutes; remove from pan at once.

Biscuits

2 level cups of unsifted flour	1 tablespoon lard or butter
1 tablespoon baking powder	1 cup sweet milk
½ level teaspoon salt	

Sift flour, baking powder and salt together. Cut shortening in with spatula or mixing spoon. Add sweet milk, stir briskly, roll out on floured board, cut and bake in quick oven.

Coffee Cake

Flour sifted 1½ cups
Baking powder 1 level teaspoon
Salt ¼ teaspoon
Milk ½ cup
Egg 1

Sugar ½ cup
Melted butter 1 tablespoon
Currants 1 cup
Cinnamon

Combine all dry materials and sift. To this add combined milk, beaten egg, sugar and melted butter. Beat well; pour into shallow greased baking pan; sprinkle with sugar, cinnamon, currants, and dots of butter. Bake twenty-five minutes in moderate oven.

Jumbles

1 cup butter
1 cup sugar
4 eggs

2 cups flour
½ teaspoon baking powder

Rub together the butter and sugar; add the beaten eggs and flour sifted with the powder; flour the board, roll out the dough rather thin, cut with jumble cutter or any you might have; roll in sugar, lay out on greased tin; bake in fairly hot oven 10 minutes.

Sand Tarts

1 cup butter
3 eggs, whites and yolks beaten separately
1 tablespoonful water

1½ cups sugar

½ teaspoonful baking powder
mixed in enough flour to make
stiff enough to roll

Roll out thin, cut in separate squares, sprinkle sugar and cinnamon on top, and bake.

Lemon Chiffon Pie

¾ cup sugar

Yolks of 2 eggs

3 tablespoonfuls lemon juice

1 tablespoonful melted butter or butter substitute

¾ cup water

½ teaspoonful salt

3 tablespoonfuls flour

Grated rind of 1 lemon

¼ cup condensed milk

Whites of 2 eggs

Mix flour and sugar, add egg yolks, slightly beaten, grated rind, butter substitute, water, milk, and lemon juice. Fold in stiffly beaten whites and salt. Fill piecrust and bake until firm in moderate oven. Number served, 6 persons.

Chocolate Bavarian Cream

1 envelope gelatin

1 cup cream

2 tablespoons boiling water

1 - 2 cups sugar

1 - 2 oz. grated chocolate

1 egg

1 cup milk

Vanilla

Cook in a double boiler the milk, well-beaten egg, sugar, and grated chocolate, until the chocolate is melted and well mixed. Remove from fire and add gelatin, which has been rubbed to a smooth paste in the boiling water, and set in a cool place to jelly. When beginning to cool, fold in cream whipped; flavor with vanilla and set in a cool place. Two tablespoons of cocoa may be used and mixed dry with gelatin and sugar. Moisten with the hot milk to make a paste and then add to the remainder. Cook five minutes stirring constantly.

Devil's Food Cake

3 squares unsweetened chocolate   2 tablespoons sugar
1½ teaspoons milk   4 tablespoons shortening
1 cup sugar   2 eggs
⅔ cup milk   1⅓ cups flour
2 teaspoons baking powder   ⅛ teaspoon salt

Cook slowly until smooth first three ingredients. Cream shortening; add sugar and beat well. Add yolks of eggs and beat again. Stir in chocolate mixture and then add alternately the milk and flour which has been sifted with the baking powder and salt. Fold in the beaten whites of eggs. Bake in greased loaf pan in moderate oven 50 to 60 minutes. Cover with white or chocolate icing.

Sea Foam Icing

1 cup brown sugar   White of one egg
⅓ cup water   1 teaspoon baking powder

Boil sugar and water without stirring until syrup spins a thread. Add hot syrup slowly to beaten egg white, beating continually, preferably on platter with wire whip. Add baking powder. When icing foams, put between layers and on top of cake.

Silver Cake

2 cups sugar

½ teaspoon salt

1 teaspoon almond extract

1 cup milk

4 cups flour

2 teaspoons baking powder

6 whites of eggs

⅔ cup butter

Cream the butter and sugar, add alternately the milk and flour mixed with salt and baking powder; then the extract and the stiffly whipped whites. Beat well and bake in loaf pan in moderate oven.

Cottage Pudding

2¼ cups sifted flour

¼ teaspoon salt

1 egg

¾ cup sugar

4 level teaspoons baking powder

1 cup milk

4 tablespoons butter

1 teaspoon vanilla

Combine all dry materials and sift. Separate egg. Cream butter and sugar together; add combined egg yolk and milk alternately with combined dry material; fold in stiffly beaten whites of egg. Place in shallow cake tin. Bake for half hour in moderate oven. Serve with Hard Sauce.

Hard Sauce

⅓ cup butter

1 teaspoon vanilla

1 cup powdered sugar

Cream butter; add sugar gradually; then vanilla. Beat until sauce is fluffy and smooth.

STRAWBERRY SHORT CAKE

Strawberry Short Cake

2 cups bread flour	4 teaspoons baking powder
½ teaspoon salt	1 tablespoon sugar
⅓ cup of butter	¾ cup milk

Mix and sift the dry ingredients twice. Work in the butter with the tips of the fingers and add enough milk gradually to make as soft a dough as possible and still one that will not stick to the floured board when it is tossed about. Divide the dough in two parts and roll out each half to fit a round layer-cake tin which has been well greased. Bake in a hot oven for 10 or 25 minutes. Butter the under crust and spread with sweetened mashed berries. (Use one cup of sugar to a box of berries.) Cover the top with sifted powdered sugar, or cover the top with whipped cream, which should be sweetened with a heaping tablespoon of powdered sugar and ¼ teaspoon of vanilla.

Charlotte Russe

1 pint cream
¼ cup powdered sugar

1 teaspoon vanilla extract
Ladyfingers

Mix ingredients. Have very cold and whip to stiff froth. Line dish with sponge cake or ladyfingers, fill with whipped cream and serve cold.

Maple Parfait

1¼ cup maple syrup
4 eggs

2½ cups heavy cream
1 cup chopped pecans

Heat maple syrup and stir slowly into beaten eggs. Whip cream stiff and add. Partially freeze, then stir in thoroughly the pecans chopped very fine. Finish freezing.

Caramel Ice Cream

1 pint milk
1 - 2 pound sugar
1 quart cream

1 tablespoonful extract of vanilla
Pint of whipped cream (optional)

Put a quarter of a pound of white or brown sugar, with two teaspoonfuls of water, in a frying pan. Stir til it melts and becomes of a dark brown color. Turn the burnt sugar into the milk, stir over the fire for a minute, and let cool. When cold add the sugar, cream and flavoring extract, mix thoroughly and freeze. This is improved by the addition of a pint of whipped cream when frozen.

Hot Chocolate Sauce

2 squares chocolate   1 cup corn syrup
2 cups water   Vanilla
3 cups sugar

Boil two squares chocolate in two cups water. When entirely dissolved, add three cups sugar and one cup corn syrup. Flavor with vanilla. This is for pouring over ice cream.

Fudge

3 cups sugar   1 cup milk
1 tablespoonful butter   3 tablespoonfuls chocolate
                     1 - 2 teaspoonful vanilla extract

When the sugar is melted, add chocolate and boil about one quarter hour. Then remove from the fire, adding the vanilla, and pour upon buttered dish to be divided into convenient shapes.

Angel Food Cake

Whites of 8 eggs   ½ teaspoon cream of tartar
1¼ cups of granulated sugar   1 cup flour
Pinch of salt   ¾ teaspoon vanilla

Sift the flour four times before measuring. Add salt to eggs than whip until frothy. Add cream of tartar and continue beating until eggs are stiff and dry, then add sugar gradually. Add flavoring and lastly fold the flour lightly and thoroughly through the mixture. Bake 45 minutes in a moderate oven in an unbuttered angel cake pan.

Popovers

2 cups flour
2 eggs

½ teaspoon salt
2 cups milk

Sift together flour and salt. Make a well in flour, break eggs into well, add milk and stir until smooth. Pour into hot, greased gem pans and bake 25 to 35 minutes in very hot oven. If taken out of oven too soon they will fall.

Molasses Doughnuts

1 cup molasses
½ cup milk
1 teaspoonful soda
¼ teaspoonful cloves

1 cup shortening, melted
1½ cups bread flour
½ teaspoonful ginger
¼ teaspoonful cinnamon

Mix the molasses and shortening, add milk and flour, mixed and sifted with the soda and spices. Beat until smooth. Bake in gem pans.

Cocoa Snaps

4 tablespoonfuls cocoa
2 cupfuls of flour
½ teaspoonful of ginger
¼ teaspoonful of allspice
1 teaspoonful of baking powder

¼ cupful of sugar
4 tablespoonfuls of lard
½ cupful of molasses
4 tablespoonfuls of water
¼ teasponful of soda

Melt the shortening and stir into it the cocoa, add the water, sugar, and molasses. Stir the flour, ginger, allspice, soda, and baking powder into the rest of the ingredients. Chill the dough and roll out on a floured board as thin as possible, cut into fancy shapes or rounds, and bake in buttered pan in a moderate oven.

Scotch Cakes

1 pound flour
½ pound butter
½ teaspoon baking powder

⅔ cup granulated sugar
1 teaspoon extract vanilla
Caraway seeds

Mix flour and baking powder. Rub in butter as for biscuits. Work in the sugar and flavoring. This gives a rather crumbly dough. Work with hands to make it adhere, pat out in cakes, sprinkle with caraway seeds. Bake in moderate oven. Very rich.

Fig Envelopes

2 cups flour	2 teaspoons shortening
3 teaspoons baking powder	⅔ cup milk
½ teaspoon salt	1 cup chopped figs
2 tablespoons sugar	1 egg

Sift together flour, baking powder, salt, and sugar; add shortening and mix in very lightly; add enough milk to form soft dough. Dust board with flour and roll out dough ¼-inch thick, cut into squares and on each piece put one tablespoon of fig; brush edges with cold milk; fold like an envelope and press edges together. Brush tops with egg beaten with one tablespoon milk and one teaspoon sugar. Bake about 20 minutes in hot oven.

Cocoa Pie

4 tablespoonfuls of cocoa	½ cupful of sugar
3 tablespoonfuls of cornstarch	¼ teaspoonful of salt
1 tablespoonful of butter substitute	2 cupfuls of milk
2 eggs	1 teaspoonful of vanilla

Melt the butter substitute and stir in the cocoa and cornstarch, add the yolks of the eggs well beaten, the sugar, salt and milk. Cook in top of double boiler until thick, stirring constantly. Pour into well baked pie crust and cover with meringue made by beating the whites of the eggs until stiff and adding two tablespoonfuls of sugar. Brown lightly in the oven, and serve cold.

INTRODUCTION

I STARTED COLLECTING VINTAGE RECIPE BOOKLETS OVER A DECADE AGO IN BROOKLYN. My then toddler-aged son and I had just dropped off his older brother at art class, when we stumbled upon a nearby antique/junk shop. The shop's door was open, and as I pushed the stroller past and peered in, several boxes filled with brightly colored antique recipe pamphlets, illustrated with baked goods and baking ingredients, caught my eye. I had recently started working as a junior baker at the hot, new Brooklyn bakery, Baked, and I was completely preoccupied with baking, eating, and reading about all things sweet. The pamphlets looked like they'd be right up my old-school-dessert-obsessed alley.

I had to move quickly, as the shop was no place for a stroller or its inhabitant, so I scooped up a handful of the booklets with the most inviting covers, paid, and departed. Once home, I discovered that my instinct had been right: not only did I love the period illustrations, both within the pages of the pamphlets as well as on their covers, but the booklets included recipes for all of the desserts I loved best: layer cakes with billowy frosting, cream pies with meringue topping, yeasted cinnamon buns, fritters, and caramel popcorn, to name a few.

Using my research skills, honed during my pre-baking days as a lawyer, I soon discovered that vintage recipe booklets were distributed from the late-nineteenth to the mid-twentieth century to America's housewives by brand-name ingredient and kitchen appliance companies. Heckers Flour and Frigidaire, for instance, offered a booklet upon the purchase of a bag of flour or a refrigerator. In light of their original content and distinctive look, the booklets proved to be a uniquely powerful advertising tool. They helped companies sell their products via recipes, tips for how best to work with the ingredient or appliance, engaging and brightly colored cover art, and promises to the housewife of fortitude in the kitchen, and a happily satiated husband.

The marketing message of the booklets changed, I learned, depending on the decade in which they were distributed. Booklets from the early 1900s, influenced by the 1906 passage of the Federal Pure Food and Drug Act, regulating food safety, advised women to keep their families healthy by baking with the "pure" and "healthy" ingredient advertised within their pages. During the Great Depression, those of the 1930s appealed to the housewife's frugal nature and sense of convenience. They implored her, for instance, to save money *and* time by leavening her cakes or waffles with baking powder, as opposed to doing so the old-fashioned way, with eggs or yeast. Finally, the booklets of the 1950s, the salad days of the housewife, as it were, emphasized how dazzling the life of the booklet-wielding homemaker might be, encouraging her to bake "delicious, *glamorous* cakes" and to tell her neighbors of the fabulous ingredient she'd been introduced to so "that they [too might] enjoy luxurious living."

Needless to say, the more I learned about the booklets, the more enamored I became, and soon the collecting of recipe pamphlets began in earnest—as did the baking from their pages. The recipes themselves proved to be simple, basically foolproof, and the perfect canvas for twisting and tweaking. For instance, recipes from the booklets of the early 1900s lacked any imagination, or bold flavors, and called for nothing but the most obvious of ingredients. Those distributed fifty years later tended to rely on more processed, fewer fresh, ingredients, such as canned fruits in sugary syrups, than what we bake with today. But with the addition of an unexpected spice or extract, a different kind of milk or flour, a bit of extra salt, more butter than shortening, and a little less food coloring, I found I could modernize the recipes to appeal to the more adventurous, accepting, and global palate of today's home bakers, while still remaining true to their old-school roots. In so doing, a passion for recipe development materialized that I hadn't a clue existed.

Now, more than ten years later, I have been fortunate enough to morph my passion into a profession, and I'm still just as smitten with vintage recipe booklets as I was the day I bought my first few in that junk shop. This book brings together my passion for revamping recipes, born from those early days of vintage recipe booklet collecting, and the collection itself. The vast majority of my booklet recipes are for fabulous old-school treats, such as biscuits and doughnuts, snack cakes and refrigerator desserts, ice cream and fudge. They all take beautifully to a gentle nudge into the twenty-first century with a tweak here—via an "everything" seasoning blend, and a twist there—via a glug of booze, or a handful of fresh basil.

For instance, to a very minimalist popover, I have added pecorino romano cheese and freshly ground black pepper *(PAGE 33)*. To the ever-popular fritter, I have added a chai spice blend *(PAGE 18)*. To the ladyfingers in my charlotte russe (a precursor to the icebox cake), I have added fresh thyme *(PAGE 128)*. My take on caramels includes a sprinkling of salt and pepper *(PAGE 155)*.

I picked recipes from booklets published between the late 1800s and the 1950s (with one or two from the 1960s and 1970s if I found the booklet cover particularly swoon-worthy, or the recipes within it particularly deserving of a modern makeover), as the vast majority of booklets were published during this fifty-year era, and are well represented in my collection. Within that time period, I have revamped those recipes that turned up in booklet after booklet, such as coffee cake, fig cookies, chiffon pie, strawberry shortcake, and candied nuts, to name a few. Modernizing the most popular recipes proved especially gratifying, as these simple favorites take so well to the twenty-first-century baker's infatuation with ingredients like intensely flavored spices, fresh herbs, nut milks, and alternative flours.

But I included less popular recipes, as well. Recipes from Swedish tea rolls to meringue cradle cake, potato chip balls, and graham cracker fruit crisp appeal simply because they are unique and whimsical on their face. Modern bakers have an appetite for the adventure and challenge of trying something new and different, and I was eager to satiate it with the handful of recipes I've included here.

Vintage booklet recipes provide an exceptional springboard for twisting and tweaking due to their simplicity *and* reliability. If you are a collector yourself, I hope you find that I have done the recipes the delicious justice they deserve. If you are new to the world of early to mid-century recipe pamphlets, welcome. You may never leave.

№ 1

Sweet & Savory Morning Treats

"ANY MAN GETS TIRED OF TOAST ALL THE TIME."

— Davis Master Pattern Baking Formulas (1938)

VINTAGE ADVICE FOR THE MODERN KITCHEN

For those attempting thermometer-free frying, check your oil temperature via a cube of white bread—the oil is at proper temperature for frying doughnuts/fritters, 350° to 375°F [180° to 190°C], when the cube browns in 40 seconds.

MOLASSES DOUGHNUTS WITH CHOCOLATE-GINGER GLAZE

MAKES 12 DOUGHNUTS AND LOADS OF HOLES

Grandma's Old Fashioned Molasses Recipes (1928) includes three *different* recipes for molasses dough-nuts, an indication of just how fond folks were of this treat. I have revamped the recipe for Sour Milk ones, using yeast instead of baking soda, resulting in doughnuts that are light and fluffy. Like the originals, my recipe does not include sugar, allowing the molasses flavor to truly shine. The chocolate-ginger glaze on one side of the doughnut and the cinnamon-sugar coating on the other ensures your sweet tooth won't miss it.

DOUGHNUTS

3 cups [420 g]
all-purpose flour

2¾ tsp instant yeast

¼ cup [45 g]
potato starch

1½ tsp table salt

1 tsp ground ginger

¾ tsp ground cinnamon

3 Tbsp vegetable shortening

1 cup [240 ml] buttermilk,
at room temperature

⅓ cup [105 g] molasses

1 egg, at room temperature

CONT'D

Grease a medium bowl with vegetable oil or nonstick cooking spray. Line 2 rimmed baking sheets with parchment paper. Line a wire rack with a thick layer of paper towels or 1 or 2 large paper grocery bags and set near the cooktop.

FOR THE DOUGHNUTS In the bowl of a stand mixer fitted with the paddle attachment, combine the flour, yeast, starch, salt, ginger, and cinnamon and mix on low speed until a shaggy dough forms. Add the shortening, buttermilk, molasses, and egg and continue to mix until mostly incorporated.

Remove the paddle and replace with the dough hook attachment. On medium speed, knead the dough until a smooth(ish) mass forms that comes off the sides of the bowl, 5 to 7 minutes. If the dough is very sticky, add a little extra flour. Alternatively, if it's too dry, add a little buttermilk, until it sticks just a bit.

CONT'D

CINNAMON-SUGAR

6 Tbsp [90 g] granulated sugar

¾ tsp ground cinnamon

CHOCOLATE-GINGER GLAZE

1½ cups [180 g] confectioners' sugar, sifted

¼ cup [20 g] Dutch-process cocoa powder, sifted

½ cup [120 ml] heavy cream

1 Tbsp pure vanilla extract

½ to 1 tsp ground ginger

½ to ¾ tsp ground cinnamon

Vegetable oil for frying

Transfer the dough to the prepared bowl and turn it to coat with oil. Cover the bowl with plastic wrap and set aside in a warm place for 1 to 1½ hours, until it has practically doubled in size.

If it feels too sticky to work with, lightly flour the counter and turn the dough out onto it. With a rolling pin, roll out the dough until it is about ½ in [12 cm] thick. Using a 3-in [7.5-cm] round cookie cutter for the doughnut, and a 1-in [2.5-cm] or smaller one for the hole, begin cutting out doughnuts and holes, dipping the cutters in flour each time you do so, if the dough is sticky. Carefully transfer them to the prepared baking sheets as you work, using your hands or a large spatula. Do not reroll the scraps (make additional holes instead). Cover the sheets with plastic wrap, and set aside for 30 to 45 minutes in a warm place, or until the doughnuts rise to about 1½ times their original size.

FOR THE CINNAMON-SUGAR Combine the sugar and cinnamon in a small bowl and set aside.

FOR THE GLAZE Place all of the glaze ingredients in a medium bowl and whisk to combine, adding more heavy cream, if you'd like a thinner glaze.

Fill a large heavy saucepan with 2 in [5 cm] of oil. Attach a deep-fat/candy thermometer to the side of the pan and heat the oil on medium-high heat until the temperature reaches 350°F [180°C].

Have the paper towel–lined wire rack near your pan. Carefully lower a doughnut into the oil using a wire skimmer or slotted spoon. Fry for about 2 minutes total, gently flipping after 1 minute. The doughnut holes will cook through in even less time, so you may want to cook all of the doughnuts first and then the holes. Depending on the size of your pan and your patience level, you may fry one doughnut at a time, or many.

Carefully transfer the doughnuts to the prepared wire rack. To prevent the doughnuts from absorbing extra oil, gently pat them with additional paper towels.

Let the doughnuts cool for 5 minutes before dipping one side of the bottom half of each one in the cinnamon-sugar mixture and the other side in the glaze. For a nice, thick glaze, I *highly* recommend double-dipping once the first coat is set. Place the doughnuts back on the rack, sugar-side down, while the glaze sets a bit before serving.

The doughnuts are best enjoyed warm, immediately after frying.

CHAI BANANA FRITTERS

MAKES 24 FRITTERS

Fritters were a popular treat in the first half of the twentieth century, particularly apple, but banana did make an appearance on occasion. I love bananas *and* all things fried, so here is my version of a banana fritter. It is a take-off of the one from *The Little Book of Excellent Recipes* (1934), but with a modern and spicy kick of chai spice blend, plus a touch of sweetness via a little brown sugar—so delicious with bananas. My *Bananas . . . How to Serve Them* (1942) booklet recommends serving banana fritters for dinner, with roast beef and buttered cauliflower. I, however, prefer them for breakfast or dessert. I'll let you make the final call.

3 Tbsp light
brown sugar

1 cup [140 g]
all-purpose flour

½ cup [70 g] cornstarch

1 tsp baking powder

¾ tsp table salt

1 tsp ground cardamom

¾ tsp ground ginger

½ tsp ground cinnamon

¼ tsp ground cloves

¼ tsp ground nutmeg

¼ tsp ground allspice

½ cup [120 ml] whole milk,
at room temperature

1 Tbsp unsalted butter,
melted and cooled

Line a wire rack with a thick layer of paper towels or 1 or 2 large paper grocery bags and set near the cooktop.

In a medium bowl, whisk together the brown sugar, flour, cornstarch, baking powder, salt, cardamom, ginger, cinnamon, cloves, nutmeg, and allspice.

In a large bowl, whisk together the milk, melted butter, egg, yolk, and vanilla until frothy. Fold the dry ingredients into the milk mixture, using a rubber spatula, until just a few streaks of flour remain. Let the batter rest in the refrigerator, covered with plastic wrap, for 2 hours, or up to overnight.

Fold in the bananas just to combine, taking care not to mash them. Ideally, you want chunks of banana in your fritters.

Fill a large heavy saucepan with 2 in [5 cm] of oil. Attach a deep-fat/candy thermometer to the side of the pan and heat the oil on medium-high heat until the temperature reaches 350°F [180°C].

1 egg

1 egg yolk

2 tsp pure vanilla extract

1½ to 2 ripe bananas,
cut into small pieces

Vegetable oil for frying

6 Tbsp [90 g]
granulated sugar

¾ tsp ground cinnamon

Scoop 1- to 1½-tablespoon balls of batter, using a cookie scoop or measuring spoon, and place them in the oil. Fry the fritters for 2 to 3 minutes total, gently flipping them over with wooden chopsticks or any two thin utensils at the halfway point, once one side has browned. Depending on the size of your pan and your patience level, you may fry one fritter at a time or many.

Using a slotted spoon, carefully transfer the fritters to the prepared wire rack. To prevent the fritters from absorbing extra oil, gently pat them with additional paper towels.

Combine the granulated sugar and cinnamon in a small bowl. Once the fritters are cool enough to handle, toss each one in the mixture until coated. Fritters are best enjoyed warm on the day they are made.

BUTTERSCOTCH PECAN CURLS

MAKES 8 CURLS

Sticky bun recipes come with many different names: rolls, curls, curlicues, and more. I am a sucker for a cute name, so in my book (quite literally) they will be forever called "curls." I started with the recipe for Royal Cinnamon Buns from *The Little Gingerbread Man* (1923), substituting yeast for the baking powder, because a yeasted "curl" is one of life's tastiest pleasures. I made sure to include an unusually generous amount of cinnamon (recipes from the 1920s used spices sparingly, if at all) and I added even more spice to the filling, including cayenne, to impart a twenty-first-century kick.

DOUGH

1¾ cups [245 g]
bread flour

1¼ tsp instant yeast

2 Tbsp granulated sugar

2 Tbsp potato starch

¾ tsp table salt

2 Tbsp unsalted butter, at room temperature

1 egg, at room temperature

½ cup [120 ml] buttermilk, at room temperature

BUTTERSCOTCH SAUCE

2 Tbsp unsalted butter

6 Tbsp [90 g]
packed light brown sugar

6 Tbsp [90 ml]
heavy cream

CONT'D

Grease a medium bowl with vegetable oil or nonstick cooking spray. Grease a round 9-in [23-cm] cake pan with nonstick cooking spray or softened butter.

FOR THE DOUGH In the bowl of a stand mixer fitted with the paddle attachment, combine the flour, yeast, granulated sugar, starch, and salt and mix until incorporated. Add the butter, egg, and buttermilk and beat on medium-low speed until a shaggy dough forms.

Replace the paddle with the dough hook attachment, increase the speed to medium, and continue to beat the dough until a smooth mass forms that comes off the sides of the bowl and sticks only a bit to the bottom, 4 to 6 minutes. If the dough is very sticky, add a little extra flour. Alternatively, if it's too dry, add a bit of buttermilk, until it sticks just a bit.

CONT'D

2 Tbsp light corn syrup

½ tsp table salt

½ tsp ground cinnamon

¼ tsp ground cardamom

1 cup [140 g]
chopped pecans, toasted
(see page 168)

FILLING
½ cup [110 g]
unsalted butter, melted

3 Tbsp all-purpose flour

5 Tbsp [65 g]
packed light brown sugar

5 Tbsp [65 g]
granulated sugar

½ tsp table salt

1½ tsp ground cinnamon

½ tsp ground ginger

¼ tsp ground cardamom

¼ tsp ground nutmeg

¼ tsp cayenne
pepper, optional

Flaky sea salt for sprinkling

Transfer the dough to the prepared bowl and turn it to coat in oil. Cover the bowl with plastic wrap and set aside in a warm place for 1 to 1½ hours, until it has practically doubled in size.

FOR THE SAUCE Combine all of the ingredients except the pecans in a small saucepan over medium to medium-high heat. Bring to a boil, decrease the heat, and simmer for 3 to 5 minutes. Pour the sauce into the bottom of the prepared pan and sprinkle with about two-thirds of the pecans in a single layer. Set the rest of the nuts aside.

FOR THE FILLING Combine 7 tablespoons [100 g] of the melted butter with the rest of the filling ingredients in a bowl and whisk until a spreadable paste forms. Let the filling sit on the counter to come to room temperature and firm up a bit before using, at least 20 minutes.

If the dough feels too sticky to work with, lightly flour the counter before turning the dough out onto it. Using your hands, shape the dough into a rectangle, with the longest side closest to you. With a rolling pin, or your hands, create a rectangle, roughly 9 in by 14 in [23 cm by 33 cm] and about ½ in [12 mm] thick.

Brush the rectangle with the remaining melted butter. Using a small offset spatula or a butter knife, spread the filling in an even layer all the way to the edges of the rectangle. Sprinkle with the remaining pecans and press them into the filling with your hands. Begin rolling on the long side of the rectangle up and away from you, into a cylinder shape. Roll it as tightly and evenly as you can.

With a sharp knife, cut the cylinder into 8 equal pieces and place in the prepared pan, cut-side up, pressing them into the butterscotch sauce and being mindful not to crowd them. Tightly wrap the pan in plastic wrap and refrigerate overnight. The next morning, let the curls sit at room temperature for about 30 to 45 minutes before removing the plastic and baking.

Or, if you want to bake them right away, loosely cover the pan with plastic wrap and set aside in a warm place for 30 to 45 minutes, or until the curls rise to about 1½ times their original size.

Preheat the oven to 375°F [190°C].

Bake until the curls are nicely browned, with an internal temperature of 200°F [95°C], 30 to 35 minutes. Check them at about 28 minutes and if they are too dark, tent with foil. If not using a thermometer, stick a paring knife between the curls and poke around a bit, to ensure the dough is fully cooked.

Transfer the pan to a wire rack, let cool for 10 minutes, and invert them onto a serving platter, being sure to scrape any excess sauce from the pan onto the top of the curls. Let cool for 10 minutes more. Sprinkle with flaky sea salt, pour yourself a cup of coffee, and enjoy.

These are best eaten the day they are baked, either warm or at room temperature, but they can be reheated the next day in a pinch. Simply wrap in aluminum foil and place in a 350°F [1850°C] oven for 20 minutes, or until warmed through.

CINNAMON-RAISIN FLAKE-APART BREAD

SERVES 12

The Pillsbury Bake-Off, a cooking contest that ran annually between 1949 and 1976, and has occurred more sporadically since, required all of its contestants to use Pillsbury flour. Mrs. Paul W. Strobel's Buttercrust Flake-Aparts recipe was in *Pillsbury's 2nd Grand National 100 Prizewinning Recipes* (1951) and calls for a yeasted dough cut into squares, layered, and placed in a muffin tin. I added potato starch to help with handling and shaping the dough and used a loaf pan instead of a muffin tin. The cinnamon-sugar, raisins, and melted butter filling was inspired by the victory buns in *Sun-Maid Raisins: Their Food Value and 92 Selected Recipes* (1921).

DOUGH

2 cups [280 g] all-purpose flour

1 cup [140 g] bread flour

2½ tsp instant yeast

¼ cup [50 g] granulated sugar

1½ tsp table salt

¼ cup [45 g] potato starch

3 Tbsp unsalted butter, at room temperature

1 cup [240 ml] whole milk, at room temperature

1 egg, at room temperature

CONT'D

Grease a medium bowl with vegetable oil or nonstick cooking spray. Grease a 9-in-by-5-in [23-cm-by-12-cm] loaf pan with nonstick cooking spray or softened butter. Line the bottom and two short sides with parchment paper and grease again.

FOR THE DOUGH In the bowl of a stand mixer fitted with the paddle attachment, combine the all-purpose and bread flours, yeast, sugar, salt, and potato starch and mix until incorporated. Add the butter, milk, and egg and mix on medium-low speed until a shaggy dough forms.

Replace the paddle with the dough hook attachment. On medium-high speed, knead the dough until a smooth mass forms that comes off the sides of the bowl and sticks only a bit to the bottom, 5 to 7 minutes. If the dough is very sticky, add a little extra flour. Alternatively, if it's too dry, add a bit of milk, until it sticks just a bit.

CONT'D

FILLING

1 Tbsp ground cinnamon

1 cup [200 g] granulated sugar

¼ cup [55 g] unsalted butter, melted

¾ cup [105 g] raisins

Transfer the dough into the prepared bowl. Cover the bowl with plastic wrap, and set aside in a warm place for 1 to 1½ hours, until it has practically doubled in size.

FOR THE FILLING In a small bowl, whisk the cinnamon and sugar to combine. Set aside.

If the dough feels too sticky to work with, lightly flour the counter before turning the dough out onto it. Using your hands, shape the dough into a rectangle, with the longest side closest to you. With a rolling pin or your hands, form a rectangle roughly 20 in by 15 in [50 cm by 38 cm].

Generously brush the dough with the melted butter (you will have some left over). Evenly sprinkle the raisins over the dough, pressing them in with your fingers. Top with the cinnamon-sugar mixture.

Using a bench scraper or sharp knife, cut the rectangle the long way into 6 equal strips. Stack the 6 strips on top of each other and cut the layered strips the short way into 6 equal pieces. Stack the 36 pieces upright in the prepared pan, like you would slices of bread, or dominoes. The raisins will fall off as you do this, just stick them back into the dough or sprinkle them on top of the loaf.

Tightly wrap the pan in plastic wrap and refrigerate overnight. The next morning, let the bread sit at room temperature for about 30 to 45 minutes before removing the plastic and baking.

Or, if you want to bake right away, loosely cover the pan with plastic wrap and set aside in a warm place for 30 to 45 minutes, or until the bread rises to about 1½ times its original size.

Preheat the oven to 375°F [190°C].

Bake the bread until nicely browned, 40 to 45 minutes. Tent the loaf with aluminum foil at the 35-minute mark, to keep the top of the loaf from getting too brown. The bread is done when its internal temperature is 200°F [95°C]. If you do not have a thermometer, stick a paring knife in between the "flakes" to confirm that the dough is cooked through.

Transfer the pan to a wire rack and brush the top with the extra melted butter. Let cool until the pan is easy to handle, remove the loaf, and let it cool, right-side up, on a wire rack. Serve warm.

The bread is best the day it is made, but can be stored, tightly wrapped in plastic wrap, on the counter for up to 3 days. Toasting the day-old bread is awfully nice, too.

SWEDISH TEA ROLLS

MAKES 36 ROLLS

Swedish Tea Rolls taste like the best mini cinnamon-sugar toaster pastry you've ever had. Three different General Foods booklets have recipes for them, but after baking those from *The Calumet Baking Book* (1931), I knew they deserved a twenty-first-century makeover. A little heavy cream made for a richer-tasting pastry, and extra cinnamon and sugar gave the filling extra punch. Brushing the tops with an egg wash and sprinkling with turbinado sugar added shine, color, and crunch. The perfect treat for breakfast or with an afternoon cup of tea.

PASTRY DOUGH

2 cups [240 g] cake flour

2 tsp baking powder

½ tsp table salt

½ cup [110 g] unsalted butter, chilled

⅔ cup [160 ml] heavy cream

FILLING

¾ cup [150 g] granulated sugar

2½ tsp ground cinnamon

3 Tbsp unsalted butter, melted

EGG WASH

1 egg

Splash of heavy cream

Turbinado sugar for sprinkling

Line a rimmed baking sheet with parchment paper and set aside.

FOR THE DOUGH Combine the flour, baking powder, and salt in the bowl of a food processor fitted with the metal blade and process briefly to combine. Cut the butter into cubes, add to the flour mixture, and pulse until it is the consistency of coarse meal. Add the heavy cream slowly, pulsing as you do so. Once the dough comes together, stop the processor.

Portion the dough into tablespoon-size balls, place on the prepared baking sheet, cover tightly with plastic wrap, and refrigerate for 2 hours or up to 1 day.

FOR THE FILLING Combine the sugar and cinnamon in a small bowl. Place the melted butter in another small bowl.

Working with one ball at a time, roll in the cinnamon-sugar mixture and, on a work surface, roll it flat with a rolling pin, or press with your hands, into a 3-in [7.5-cm] round, sprinkling with more cinnamon sugar if sticky. Brush with the melted butter and place a

rounded ½ teaspoon of the cinnamon-sugar mixture in the center of the round. Flour your fingers and gently fold the round in half, pressing gently to seal, and place on the prepared sheet. Repeat with the remaining balls, spacing them evenly.

Cover tightly with plastic wrap and freeze for at least 1 hour or up to 3 days before baking.

Preheat the oven to 400°F [200°C].

FOR THE EGG WASH Combine the egg and cream in a small bowl. Brush the wash on each roll. Sprinkle with turbinado sugar and bake for 15 to 17 minutes, rotating at the halfway point, until the rolls are lightly browned. Serve warm or at room temperature.

Swedish tea rolls are best enjoyed the day they are made but will keep in an airtight container on the counter for up to 3 days.

VANILLA YOGURT COFFEE CAKE

SERVES 16

Successful Baking for Flavor and Texture (1934) won me over with its gorgeous pink cover. I found a simple coffee cake recipe there and I substituted oil for the butter and added a couple of egg yolks to make it as moist as possible. With Greek yogurt so popular these days, I decided to use it instead of buttermilk—it gives the cake a wonderful tang. I also added a generous amount of vanilla (strangely, the original recipe called for none!). A buttery brown sugar-cinnamon crumb that goes both inside and on top of the cake (and can be doubled if you're all about the topping and swirl) rounds out this perfect breakfast treat.

CRUMB TOPPING AND SWIRL

½ cup [110 g] unsalted butter, melted and cooled slightly

1¼ cups [175 g] all-purpose flour

1 cup [200 g] packed dark brown sugar

1 tsp ground cinnamon

COFFEE CAKE

3¼ cups [455 g] all-purpose flour

1¼ tsp baking powder

1½ tsp baking soda

¾ tsp table salt

CONT'D

Preheat the oven to 350°F [180°C]. Generously grease a 10- to 12-cup [1.4- to 2.8-L] tube pan with nonstick cooking spray or softened butter and dust with flour, knocking out any excess.

FOR THE TOPPING AND SWIRL Mix all of the ingredients together in a medium bowl with a fork until thoroughly combined. Refrigerate, covered in plastic wrap, until ready to use.

FOR THE CAKE In a large bowl, whisk together the flour, baking powder, baking soda, and salt. In the bowl of a stand mixer fitted with the paddle attachment, beat the granulated sugar, oil, and vanilla on medium-low speed until well combined, stopping and scraping the bowl with a rubber spatula, as needed, 2 to 3 minutes. On low speed, add the eggs and yolks, one at a time, stopping and scraping the bowl after each addition.

CONT'D

2⅓ cups [465 g] granulated sugar

1 cup [240 ml] mild olive oil or vegetable oil

1 Tbsp pure vanilla extract

2 eggs

2 egg yolks

1¾ cups [420 g] plain whole Greek yogurt

Confectioners' sugar for dusting

Add the dry ingredients on low speed in three additions, alternating with two additions of the yogurt, scraping the bowl as needed with a rubber spatula. Stop the mixer and remove the bowl when there are still streaks of flour in the batter. Finish mixing by hand.

Transfer half of the batter to the prepared pan and smooth the top with a small offset spatula or butter knife. Sprinkle half of the crumb mixture evenly over the batter. Add the remaining batter and smooth the top again. Using your fingers, sprinkle the remaining crumb mixture evenly over the top of the cake, pressing down lightly.

Bake for 60 to 70 minutes, rotating the pan at the halfway point. The cake is ready when a cake tester inserted in the center comes out with a moist crumb or two. Let cool to room temperature before removing from the pan. Run a paring knife around the edges to release the cake from the pan.

Dust with confectioners' sugar before serving. The cake will keep, tightly wrapped in plastic wrap, for up to 3 days on the counter.

CACIO E PEPE POPOVERS

MAKES 6 POPOVERS

Recipes for popovers are featured in lots of booklets from those advertising baking powder to cornstarch to food mixers. The one from *Metropolitan Cook Book* (1933) calls very simply for eggs, milk, flour, salt, and shortening. With a more savory, up-to-date popover in mind, I substituted butter for the shortening and added a generous helping of finely grated pecorino romano cheese (cacio) and freshly ground black pepper (pepe). Popovers with cheese tend to have denser centers (in the most delicious of egg-y and cheese-y ways) and may not rise as much as traditional hollow-centered popovers. They are best made with room-temperature milk and eggs, and baked in a popover pan.

1 cup [140 g]
all-purpose flour

½ tsp table salt

½ tsp freshly ground
black pepper

¾ cup [45 g] finely grated
pecorino romano cheese,
plus more for sprinkling

3 eggs, at room temperature

1 cup [240 ml] whole milk,
at room temperature

2 Tbsp unsalted butter,
melted and cooled slightly

Preheat the oven to 450°F [230°C]. Generously grease a 6-cup popover pan with nonstick cooking spray or softened butter.

In a small bowl, whisk together the flour, salt, pepper, and cheese and set aside.

In a medium bowl, whisk together the eggs and milk until combined. Add the dry ingredients to the wet and whisk, just until a bit lumpy. Add the melted butter and whisk again until combined.

Place the prepared pan in the oven for 2 minutes. Remove the hot pan from the oven and pour the batter into the cups. For extra cheesy popovers, sprinkle a bit more cheese on top of each one.

CONT'D

Bake for 15 minutes. Decrease the heat to 350°F [180°C] and bake for another 15 minutes. Do not open the oven for the entire baking period. Remove the popovers from the pan and transfer to a wire rack as soon as you take them from the oven. Popovers are best enjoyed immediately, still hot with salted butter.

"EVERYTHING" BUTTERMILK BISCUITS

MAKES 8 LARGE BISCUITS

Prior to the introduction of chemical leaveners in the 1890s, biscuit recipes called for a vigorously beaten dough. But with the introduction of baking powder, making tall and tender biscuits proved effortless. The vintage recipe I started with here is from *Aristos Flour* (1910). My recipe maintains the simplicity of the original, but is given a truly modern update via the food processor (processing the dough brings "effortless" to a whole new level) and a hefty sprinkling (both in and on top of the biscuits) of "everything bagel" seasoning blend: a mixture of poppy and sesame seeds, garlic, and onion flakes.

"EVERYTHING BAGEL" SEASONING BLEND

1 Tbsp poppy seeds

1 Tbsp sesame seeds

1½ to 2 tsp dried garlic

2 tsp dried onion flakes

2 tsp kosher salt

BISCUITS

2⅔ cups [370 g] all-purpose flour

1⅓ cups [160 g] cake flour

4 tsp baking powder

1 tsp table salt

¼ tsp baking soda

Grease a 13-by-9-by-2-in [33-by-23-by-5-cm] pan with nonstick cooking spray or softened butter. Line the bottom with parchment paper.

FOR THE SEASONING BLEND Combine all of the ingredients in a small bowl. Reserve 2 to 3 tablespoons of the mix to combine with the dry ingredients, and set aside the rest for sprinkling on top of the biscuits before baking.

FOR THE BISCUITS Add the all-purpose flour, cake flour, baking powder, salt, baking soda, and the 2 to 3 tablespoons of the reserved seasoning blend to the bowl of a food processor fitted with the metal blade. Cut the butter into small cubes, add to the bowl, and pulse until the mixture resembles coarse meal. Transfer the mixture to a large bowl. Add the buttermilk and, using a wooden spoon or your hands, combine the wet into the dry until a shaggy dough forms.

1 cup [220 g] unsalted butter, chilled

1 cup plus 6 Tbsp [330 ml] buttermilk

EGG WASH

1 egg

Splash of heavy cream

Lightly flour a work surface and knead the dough a few times until it is no longer crumbly and the dry and moist bits are fully integrated. If the dough is at all sticky, lightly flour your work surface again. Gently pat or roll the dough into a rectangle at least 1½ in [4 cm] thick to ensure a tall biscuit. Using a 3-in [7.5-cm] biscuit cutter dipped in flour, begin cutting out biscuits from the dough rectangle and place in the prepared pan so they are touching (this helps them rise). You will not fill the whole pan. Collect the scraps and reroll and cut as needed.

Freeze the biscuits, tightly wrapped in plastic wrap, for at least 2 hours or, preferably, overnight. The unbaked biscuits can be frozen for up to a week.

Preheat the oven to 425°F [220°C].

FOR THE EGG WASH Combine the egg and heavy cream and brush the wash on the tops of the frozen biscuits. Sprinkle with the remaining seasoning mix. Bake for 5 minutes, decrease the heat to 400°F [200°C], and bake for about 13 minutes more, rotating the pan halfway through baking. The biscuits are ready when they are golden brown on top and lightly browned on the bottom. Let the biscuits sit a minute or two in the pan until they are easy to handle.

Biscuits are best eaten the day they are made, but can be stored, tightly wrapped in plastic wrap, on the counter for up to 3 days. To reheat, wrap them in aluminum foil and warm in a 350°F [180°C] oven for 15 to 20 minutes.

No **2**

Cookies

"HAPPY IS THE HOME WITH A FAT COOKIE JAR STUFFED FULL OF GOODIES."

— Cookies Cookies (1959)

VINTAGE ADVICE FOR THE MODERN KITCHEN

For even browning and less burning, bake your cookies on the back side of a rimmed baking sheet, which allows the hot air in your oven to more effectively circulate around your cookies.

CORNFLAKE MACAROONS WITH CHOCOLATE DRIZZLE

MAKES 16 COOKIES

My go-to chocolate-chip cookie recipe is full of Kellogg's Rice Krispies and I was over the moon to discover how frequently cookies with cereal surfaced in my booklet collection. A recipe from *55 Recipes for Hershey's Syrup* (1945) formed the base for this version of a macaroon. Adding salt to the batter proved essential (so many of these original recipes don't call for salt), and I drizzled the cookies with chocolate *after* baking, rather than combining it with the batter, allowing these cornflakes to truly shine.

3 egg whites

½ cup [100 g] granulated sugar

1½ tsp pure vanilla extract

½ tsp table salt

2½ cups [70 g] cornflakes

1½ cups [90 g] sweetened shredded coconut

Flaky sea salt for sprinkling

2 ounces [55 g] semisweet chocolate, melted (see page 169)

In a large bowl, whisk the egg whites until frothy. Add the sugar, vanilla, and salt and continue whisking until thoroughly combined and thickened. Fold the cornflakes and coconut into the egg whites using a rubber spatula. Once combined, and using your hands, crush the cornflakes in the bowl, mixing all of the ingredients together, until the mixture stays together when you squeeze it in your hand. Refrigerate for at least 2 hours or up to 3 days, covering the bowl with plastic wrap. The mixture will be much easier to scoop once it has been refrigerated.

Preheat the oven to 325°F [165°C]. Line a rimmed baking sheet with parchment paper.

Scoop 1 to 1½ tablespoons of dough with a small cookie scoop or measuring spoon, making sure to really pack the batter into the scoop/spoon. Place on the prepared pan and bake for 23 to 25 minutes, until nicely browned. Sprinkle with the sea salt and let cool.

CONT'D

Place the melted chocolate in a zippered plastic bag, cut a very tiny hole in one corner of the bag, and drizzle the chocolate over the cookies. Let the chocolate harden before serving.

The macaroons will keep in an airtight container on the counter for up to 3 days, but they get less crunchy with each day.

BUTTERSCOTCH-POTATO CHIP BALLS

MAKES 36 COOKIES

I discovered a recipe for Chip Balls in *Good Housekeeping's Book of Cookies* (1958) and realized that folks have been putting crazy add-ins like potato chips in their cookies since the mid-1950s. I'm a huge fan of cookies like this, particularly if the ingredients combine the sweet and the salty in new ways. So I took the Chip Balls recipe and added butterscotch chips, which pair with salt so beautifully. Then I quadrupled the amount of potato chips called for, rolled the balls in crushed potato chips, and finished them with a sprinkle of flaky sea salt.

2⅓ cups [325 g] all-purpose flour

1 tsp baking soda

1 tsp table salt

1 cup [180 g] butterscotch chips

1 cup [220 g] unsalted butter, melted

1 cup [200 g] packed light brown sugar

½ cup [100 g] granulated sugar

1 egg

1 egg yolk

2 tsp pure vanilla extract

CONT'D

Preheat the oven to 350°F [180°C]. Line a rimmed baking sheet with parchment paper.

In a medium bowl, combine the flour, baking soda, and salt and whisk together. Add the butterscotch chips and set aside. In the bowl of a stand mixer fitted with the paddle attachment, cream the melted butter and sugars on medium-high speed until thick, light, and glossy, 3 to 5 minutes, scraping the bowl with a rubber spatula as needed.

Decrease the mixer speed to medium-low and add the egg and yolk, one at a time, beating well and scraping the bowl after each addition with a rubber spatula. Add the vanilla and mix to combine. Add the dry ingredients all at once, mixing just to combine. Remove the bowl from the stand mixer and add 3 cups [105 g] of the potato chips to the dough, combining and crushing the chips with a rubber spatula.

CONT'D

5 cups [175 g] kettle-style
potato chips

Flaky sea salt for sprinkling

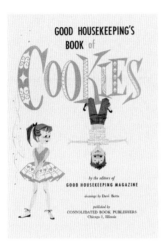

In a small bowl, crush the remaining 2 cups [70 g] potato chips. Scoop the dough into 1½-tablespoon balls with a cookie scoop or measuring spoon, rolling each ball in the leftover crushed chips, and evenly place 12 on the prepared baking sheet.

Sprinkle each cookie with flaky sea salt, and bake for 8 to 10 minutes, rotating at the halfway point, until lightly browned. Remove from the oven and press down on each cookie with a spatula to slightly flatten. Repeat with the remaining cookie dough.

Let cool briefly and serve warm, because who doesn't love a cookie warm from the oven? The cookies will keep in an airtight container on the counter for up to 3 days.

SOUR CREAM JUMBLES

MAKES 36 COOKIES

In *Betty Crocker's Picture Cook Book* (1950), jumbles are described as "little sugar cakes of old time goodness." As early as 1890 you can find recipes for them, like the one in *Royal Baker and Pastry Cook,* which features a basic recipe as well as one with peanuts. Jumbles come in a wide variety of flavors (see Jumble Variations, following), but for my version, I turned to *The Calumet Baking Book: 89 Recipes Sure to Succeed* (1929) and used sour cream instead of heavy cream to achieve the perfect balance of flavors. A roll in turbinado sugar adds a bit of crunchy contrast to the tenderness of the cookie and a final sprinkling of sanding sugar makes it sparkle.

2 cups [280 g]
all-purpose flour

½ tsp baking soda

¾ tsp baking powder

½ tsp table salt

½ cup [110 g] unsalted
butter, at room temperature

1¼ cups [250 g]
granulated sugar

2 eggs

1 Tbsp pure vanilla extract

½ cup [120 g] sour cream

1 cup [200 g] turbinado
sugar for rolling

Colored sanding sugar
for decorating

In a medium bowl, whisk together the flour, baking soda, baking powder, and salt. In the bowl of a stand mixer fitted with the paddle attachment, cream the butter and granulated sugar on medium-high speed until light and fluffy, 3 to 5 minutes.

Decrease the mixer speed to medium-low and add the eggs, one at a time, beating well and scraping the bowl after each addition with a rubber spatula. Add the vanilla and mix to combine. Add half of the flour mixture, then the sour cream, and then the other half of the flour mixture, mixing only until the last bit of flour disappears. The mixture will seem more like cake batter than cookie dough. Cover the bowl with plastic wrap and refrigerate for 2 hours or up to 3 days.

Preheat the oven to 350°F [180°C]. Line a baking sheet with parchment paper.

Place the turbinado sugar in a small bowl. As best you can (the dough will be very sticky and soft), portion

out 1 tablespoon of dough with a small cookie scoop or measuring spoon, drop each piece of dough in the turbinado sugar, and toss to coat. Roll the sugar-coated dough in your hands to form balls and evenly place on your prepared sheet. Sprinkle the balls with colored sanding sugar. Freeze for at least 1 hour or up to 1 week.

Bake for 9 to 11 minutes, rotating at the halfway point, until lightly browned around the edges. Let cool slightly on the sheet before transferring to a wire rack to cool completely. Repeat with the remaining cookie dough. The jumbles can be stored in an airtight container on the counter for up to 3 days, but they will noticeably soften each day.

JUMBLE VARIATIONS Jumbles take beautifully to different add-ins. Try adding a bit of orange zest and some mini chocolate chips; or a sprinkling of shredded sweetened coconut and a dash of coconut extract; or a handful of raisins and ½ teaspoon ground cinnamon. And for a peanut jumble? A handful of chopped roasted and salted peanuts will do just perfectly.

SAND TARTS

MAKES 24 COOKIES

I love the simplicity of Sand Tarts: cookies sprinkled with cinnamon-sugar and decorated with blanched almonds (to simulate a sand dollar). The recipe in *Davis Master Pattern Baking Formulas* (1938) was the perfect launching pad for a new version with almond flour substituted for some of the all-purpose, and almond extract to boost the nutty flavor. Rather than just sprinkle the cinnamon-sugar over the raw cookie dough balls, I recommend rolling them in it—ensuring a more intense cinnamon flavor and a lovely sandy texture. A final brush of egg white on top of the cookies helps the nuts adhere and creates a shiny and lightly browned exterior.

1 cup [140 g] all-purpose flour

1 cup [120 g] almond flour

½ tsp table salt

1 tsp baking powder

¼ tsp baking soda

½ cup [110 g] unsalted butter, at room temperature

1 cup [200 g] packed light brown sugar

1 egg

1 egg yolk

½ tsp pure vanilla extract

½ to ¾ tsp almond extract

6 Tbsp [90 g] granulated sugar

¾ tsp ground cinnamon

In a medium bowl, whisk together the all-purpose flour, almond flour, salt, baking powder, and baking soda and set aside. In the bowl of a stand mixer fitted with the paddle attachment, cream the butter and brown sugar on medium-high speed until light and fluffy, 3 to 5 minutes.

Decrease the mixer speed to medium-low and add the egg and yolk, one at a time, beating well and then scraping the bowl after each addition with a rubber spatula. Add the vanilla and almond extracts and mix to combine. Add the flour mixture, mixing just to combine. Cover the bowl with plastic wrap and refrigerate for 2 hours or, preferably, overnight. The dough will keep in the refrigerator for up to 3 days.

Preheat the oven to 350°F [180°C]. Line a baking sheet with parchment paper.

Combine the granulated sugar and cinnamon in a small bowl. Scoop 1½ tablespoons of dough with a small cookie scoop or measuring spoon, form each scoop into a ball with your hands, and roll each ball in the cinnamon-sugar, tossing to coat.

1 egg white, beaten

Sliced blanched almonds for decorating

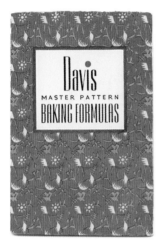

Evenly place 12 balls on your prepared sheet. Press down lightly on each ball with the bottom of a measuring cup, flattening each ball to a thick disk (don't press too hard, as the cookies do spread). Return the remaining dough to the refrigerator. Brush egg white on the tops of the flattened cookies, sprinkle on additional cinnamon-sugar, and place 3 almond slices on each cookie, simulating a sand dollar. Bake for 10 to 12 minutes, rotating at the halfway point, until lightly browned. Let cool slightly on the sheet and remove to a wire rack to cool completely. Repeat with the remaining cookie dough.

Sand Tarts will keep in an airtight container on the counter for up to 3 days.

DEEP-FRIED CARDAMOM COOKIES

MAKES 60 COOKIES

I love all things fried and was so thrilled to discover that *fattigmand*, a traditional Norwegian fried holiday cookie was prepared by housewives in their mid-twentieth-century kitchens. *Cookies: Westinghouse Christmas Cookie Cookbook* (no date) has a fattigmand recipe using nutmeg. I substituted a generous helping of cardamom, and added it to the confectioners' sugar that I sifted over the just-fried cookies for a spicier pop. Traditionally, the cookies are rolled out and cut into diamond shapes. A small cut is made in the center and one end of the diamond is pulled through the hole. To simplify, I cut them into triangles and squeeze the two long ends together.

2¼ cups [315 g]
all-purpose flour

2 tsp ground cardamom
or cinnamon

¾ tsp baking powder

¾ tsp table salt

2 eggs, at room temperature

1 egg yolk, at room
temperature

2 tsp pure vanilla extract

⅓ cup [65 g]
granulated sugar

¼ cup [55 g] unsalted
butter, melted and cooled

⅓ cup [80 ml] heavy cream,
at room temperature

Vegetable oil for frying

1 cup [120 g] confectioners'
sugar, sifted, for dusting

Line a wire rack with a thick layer of paper towels or 1 or 2 large paper grocery bags, and set near the cooktop. Line a baking sheet with parchment paper and set aside

In a medium bowl, whisk together the flour, 1½ teaspoons of the cardamom, baking powder, and salt. In a large bowl, whisk together the eggs, yolk, vanilla, and granulated sugar. Stir in the butter and the cream. Set a wire mesh sieve over the egg mixture. Sift the dry ingredients over the wet and gently fold to combine with a rubber spatula. Do not overmix: a few streaks of flour is okay.

Cover the bowl with plastic wrap and refrigerate for at least 2 hours or up to 3 days.

CONT'D

Lightly flour a work surface, and, with a rolling pin, roll the dough into an 18-in-by-12-in [30.5-cm-by-46-cm] rectangle, about ¼ in [6 mm] thick. Cut out 3-in-by-2-in [7.5-cm-by-5-cm] obtuse triangles (the kind with 2 long sides). Squeeze the ends of the two long sides of the triangle together and place on the prepared baking sheet.

Fill a large heavy saucepan with about 2 in [5 cm] of oil. Attach a deep-fat/candy thermometer to the side of the pan and heat the oil over medium-high heat until the temperature reaches 375°F [190°C].

Whisk together the remaining ½ teaspoon cardamom and the confectioners' sugar in a small bowl. Set aside.

Fry the cookies, 2 or 3 at a time, depending on the size of your saucepan—do not crowd them—for 2 to 3 minutes, flipping the cookies after about a minute, until puffy and lightly browned all over. Place the cookies on the prepared rack. Using a fine-mesh sieve, generously dust with the confectioners' sugar.

Serve immediately. Fattigmand are best served warm on the day they are made.

PEANUT BUTTER FINGERS WITH SALTY MILK CHOCOLATE GLAZE

MAKES 12 FINGERS

Nut cookies in the shape of "sticks" or "fingers" were kind of a thing back in the day. This finger recipe is inspired by the Peanut Butter Cookies in *Cookies Galore* (1956) and also the Sugared Almond Sticks in *Pillsbury's Best Butter Cookie Cookbook* (1963). I substituted bread flour for the all-purpose for chewiness, which is a must for a peanut butter cookie in my opinion. In addition, each finger is dipped in milk chocolate, because a twenty-first-century, super-chewy peanut butter cookie in the shape of a stick deserves a glaze (plus a sprinkling of flaky sea salt never hurts either).

COOKIES

1⅓ cups [185 g] bread flour

¾ tsp baking soda

½ tsp baking powder

¾ tsp table salt

½ cup [110 g] unsalted butter, at room temperature

½ cup [100 g] granulated sugar

1 cup [200 g] packed light brown sugar

6 Tbsp [90 ml] vegetable oil

1 cup [260 g] creamy peanut butter (not all-natural)

1 egg

CONT'D

Grease an 8-by-8-by-2-in [20-by-20-by-5-cm] pan with nonstick cooking spray or softened butter, line with parchment paper, leaving some overhang on the sides, and grease again.

FOR THE COOKIES In a medium bowl, whisk together the flour, baking soda, baking powder, and salt. In the bowl of a stand mixer fitted with the paddle attachment, cream the butter and sugars on medium-high speed until light and fluffy, 3 to 5 minutes. Add the oil and peanut butter and continue to mix until fully incorporated, scraping down the bowl with a rubber spatula as needed.

Decrease the mixer speed to medium-low and add the egg and yolk, one at a time, beating well and scraping the bowl after each addition with a rubber spatula. Add the vanilla and mix to combine. Add the dry ingredients all at once, mixing just to combine. Cover the bowl with plastic wrap and refrigerate for 24 to 36 hours.

CONT'D

1 egg yolk

1 Tbsp pure vanilla extract

GLAZE

3½ oz [100 g] milk chocolate

⅛ tsp table salt

¼ cup [60 ml] heavy cream

Flaky sea salt for sprinkling

Preheat the oven to 350°F [180°C].

Press the dough into the bottom of the prepared pan, making it as flat and even as possible. Bake for 22 to 27 minutes, until browned and dry to the touch. Let cool.

Freeze for about 10 minutes (this helps immeasurably with making clean cuts). Alternatively, you can tightly wrap the pan and freeze for up to a week before bringing back to room temperature and cutting and glazing.

Lift the bar cookie from the pan using the parchment paper sling. Trim off all four edges, then slice the bar in half horizontally and vertically cut each half into 6 slices, creating 12 fingers.

FOR THE GLAZE Line a baking sheet with parchment paper and set aside. Place the chocolate and salt in a small heatproof bowl. Heat the cream in a small saucepan over medium heat, until just boiling. Pour the hot cream over the chocolate and let sit for 1 minute. Mix the chocolate and cream together until the two are combined. If the chocolate is not completely melted, place in a pan set over simmering water and melt on the stove top over low heat.

Dip the top of each finger in the glaze, double-dipping for a thicker coat if you so desire, and place on the prepared baking sheet. Sprinkle flaky sea salt over each one. Refrigerate until the chocolate sets, about an hour.

Serve the fingers cold from the fridge or at room temperature. The cookies will keep in an airtight container on the counter or in the refrigerator for up to 3 days.

CHOCOLATE-MOLASSES CRINKLES

MAKES ABOUT 30 COOKIES

Recipes for ginger snaps, crinkles, and crispies pop up frequently in my booklet collection. But it was the recipe for Cocoa Snaps in *Runkel's Cocoa Delights* (no date) that I tinkered with here. My revamp includes boosting up the spices via a bit of white pepper and some ground cinnamon and substituting butter for the lard. Lard or vegetable shortening does impart chewiness in a cookie, which I love, but I wanted my cookies to have some of the flavor that only butter provides.

1½ cups [210 g]
all-purpose flour

3 Tbsp Dutch-process
cocoa powder

1½ tsp baking soda

¾ tsp table salt

1 Tbsp ground ginger

1 tsp ground cinnamon

¼ tsp ground white pepper

7 oz [200 g] semisweet
chocolate, chopped

¼ cup [80 g] molasses

1 egg

2 Tbsp light corn syrup

In a medium bowl, whisk together the flour, cocoa powder, baking soda, salt, ginger, cinnamon, and white pepper. Add the chocolate and whisk again. In a small bowl, whisk together the molasses, egg, and corn syrup.

Add the melted butter and brown sugar to the bowl of a stand mixer fitted with the paddle attachment, and mix on medium to medium-high speed until thick, light, and glossy, 3 to 5 minutes. Decrease the speed to medium-low, add the molasses mixture, and mix until combined, scraping the bowl when necessary with a rubber spatula.

Add the dry ingredients and mix until a few streaks of flour remain. Remove the bowl from the mixer and, using a rubber spatula, incorporate the remaining dry ingredients into the wet. Cover the bowl with plastic wrap and refrigerate for 24 to 36 hours.

Preheat the oven to 350°F [180°C]. Line a baking sheet with parchment paper.

½ cup [110 g] unsalted butter, melted and cooled

⅔ cup [130 g] packed dark brown sugar

Granulated sugar
for rolling

Scoop out 1½ tablespoons of dough and form into balls with your hands. Roll in granulated sugar and evenly place 12 on the prepared sheet. Return the remaining dough to the refrigerator.

Bake the cookies for 10 to 11 minutes, rotating at the halfway point. The cookies are done when they are cracking and dry-ish to the touch. After removing the cookies from the oven, press on each cookie lightly with a spatula to flatten. Repeat with the remaining cookie dough.

Serve warm or at room temperature. The cookies can be stored in an airtight container on the counter for up to 3 days.

LEMON-PEPPER SHORTBREAD

MAKES 12 COOKIES

Old-time shortbread recipes tend to be very similar and very simple—they call for lots of butter, flour, salt, sugar, and—often—caraway seeds. The one from *The Cookie Book* (1973) is reworked here, not because the recipe differed from the others, but because of its name, Scotch Shortbread. I love that the name reminds us of the cookie's provenance. Instead of the brown sugar called for in the original, I substituted both confectioners' sugar (for tenderness) *and* granulated (for a lighter color). I also added plenty of lemon zest and freshly ground black pepper for a cookie with a burst of citrus and a spicy finish.

2 cups [280 g] all-purpose flour

¾ tsp table salt

1½ to 2 tsp freshly ground black pepper

1 cup [220 g] unsalted butter, at room temperature

2 Tbsp grated lemon zest

1 Tbsp pure vanilla extract

⅓ cup [65 g] granulated sugar

⅓ cup [40 g] confectioners' sugar

Grease an 8-by-8-by-2-in [20-by-20-by-5-cm] pan with nonstick cooking spray or softened butter, line with parchment paper, and grease again.

In a medium bowl, add the flour, salt, and pepper and whisk to combine. Place the butter, zest, and vanilla in the bowl of a stand mixer fitted with the paddle attachment, and mix on medium speed until soft and light, 3 to 5 minutes. Add both sugars and continue mixing for 2 more minutes, or until fluffy, scraping down the bowl as needed.

With the mixer on low speed, slowly add the dry ingredients and mix just until a few streaks of flour remain. Remove the bowl from the mixer and continue mixing with a rubber spatula until fully combined. Transfer to the prepared pan. The dough will be quite crumbly. Drape a piece of plastic wrap over the dough and, using your hands, press the dough into the pan. Refrigerate for 2 hours or up to 3 days, tightly covered in plastic wrap. To facilitate

slicing the dough after baking, score the dough with a paring knife by lightly marking 1 horizontal line that divides the dough in half, and 6 vertical lines from top to bottom. With the tines of a fork, poke each cookie 5 times.

Preheat the oven to 350°F [180°C].

Bake for 33 to 38 minutes, rotating the pan at the halfway point. The cookies are done when they are just slightly browned and dry to the touch. Immediately cut the cookies along the scored lines. Let cool to room temperature before removing from the pan and serving (with tea or coffee, please). The cookies will keep in an airtight container on the counter for up to 3 days.

BLACK-BOTTOM BANANA DREAM BARS

MAKES 16 BARS

Dream bars are the less-layered ancestor of the seven-layer or magic bar. Here, I riffed on the Coconut Dream Squares from *Baker's Chocolate and Coconut Favorites* (1962), replacing the short-bread crust with a chocolate cookie crumb one and adding a bit of salt (like so many of the vintage recipes revamped here, the original called for none), diced banana, just a few mini chocolate chips (because . . . chocolate), and deeply toasted walnuts for good measure. The result is an awfully dreamy twenty-first-century bar, with a deliciously sticky and chewy topping.

BLACK-BOTTOM CRUST

9 oz [255 g] crisp chocolate wafer cookies

2 Tbsp granulated sugar

7 Tbsp [105 g] unsalted butter, melted

TOPPING

2 eggs

2 tsp pure vanilla extract

¾ cup [150 g] packed light brown sugar

¼ cup [30 g] cake flour

½ tsp baking powder

½ tsp table salt

1 cup [120 g] walnuts, toasted (see page 168) and finely chopped

CONT'D

Grease a 9-in-by-9-in [23-cm-by-23-cm] pan with nonstick cooking spray or softened butter. Place a piece of parchment paper on the bottom of the pan and up two sides, grease the paper, and set aside.

FOR THE CRUST Place the wafers and granulated sugar in the bowl of a food processor fitted with the metal blade and process until finely ground. Add the melted butter and process until combined, scraping down the bowl with a rubber spatula, if needed. Transfer the crumbs to the prepared pan and, using your fingers, press them evenly on the bottom of the pan. Freeze for at least 30 minutes or up to 3 days, tightly covered in plastic wrap.

Preheat the oven to 350°F [180°C].

CONT'D

1 cup [60 g] sweetened shredded coconut

1 cup [130 g] chopped ripe bananas

¼ cup [45 g] mini semisweet chocolate chips

Bake the crust for 8 to 10 minutes, rotating at the halfway point, until it is dry to the touch and slightly puffy. Let cool completely.

FOR THE TOPPING In the bowl of a stand mixer fitted with the paddle attachment, beat the eggs and vanilla on medium-high speed until quite frothy, at least 5 minutes. Add the brown sugar and beat again for 5 minutes. Remove the bowl from the mixer and, using a wire mesh sieve, sift the flour, baking powder, and salt over the bowl. Gently fold the dry ingredients into the wet with a rubber spatula. Gently fold in the walnuts, coconut, bananas, and chocolate chips.

Pour the topping over the crust and spread evenly. Bake for 20 to 25 minutes, rotating at the halfway point, until the top is nicely browned, looks set, and is no longer wet.

Let the bars come to room temperature and refrigerate until cold (this will make slicing the bars easier). Serve cold or at room temperature. The bars will keep in the refrigerator, tightly wrapped in plastic wrap, for up to 3 days.

FIG PINCUSHIONS

MAKES 48 COOKIES

If you can resist making cookies called Fig Pincushions, then you are stronger than I am. The name here has been borrowed from *Aunt Jenny's Old Fashioned Christmas Cookies* (1952), and I played with a recipe for Fruit Puffs from *Cookies Cookies* (1959). To give my cushions a richer crust, I substituted butter for the shortening and added an egg yolk. I made my own super-easy fig jam and brushed the tops with an egg wash for color. Once they were baked, I sliced them into squares, reminiscent of that most famous fig cookie in the grocery store. The result is a treat that will convert those who did not even *know* they liked fig cookies (ahem, me) into fanatics.

FIG JAM

12 oz [340 g] dried figs, stemmed and chopped

½ cup [100 g] granulated sugar

3 Tbsp freshly squeezed lemon juice

3 Tbsp boiling water, or more as needed

DOUGH

2¼ cups [315 g] all-purpose flour

1 tsp baking powder

½ tsp table salt

¾ cup [165 g] unsalted butter, at room temperature

CONT'D

FOR THE FIG JAM In a heavy-bottomed medium saucepan, combine the figs, granulated sugar, lemon juice, and 6 tablespoons [90 ml] water. Bring to a boil over medium-high heat, stirring constantly. Decrease the heat to medium and simmer for 20 minutes, stirring frequently, until the mixture thickens, adding more water if it gets too dry. Place in the jar of a blender with the boiling water. Blend until the jam is spreadable, adding additional boiling water if necessary. Transfer the jam to a container. Once at room temperature, cover and refrigerate for up to a week.

FOR THE DOUGH In a medium bowl, add the flour, baking powder, and salt and whisk together.

Add the butter, brown sugar, and granulated sugar to the bowl of a stand mixer fitted with the paddle attachment and mix on medium to medium-high speed until the mixture is light and fluffy, 3 to 5 minutes. Decrease the speed to medium-low, add the egg, yolk, and vanilla, and mix to combine.

CONT'D

⅓ cup [65 g] packed light brown sugar

⅓ cup [65 g] granulated sugar

1 egg

1 egg yolk

2 tsp pure vanilla extract

EGG WASH

1 egg

Splash of heavy cream

Turbinado sugar for sprinkling

MADE WITH PET EVAPORATED MILK

Add the dry ingredients and mix until a few streaks of flour remain. Remove the bowl from the mixer and finish mixing using a rubber spatula. Refrigerate, covered with plastic wrap, for 2 hours or up to 3 days.

Line a baking sheet with parchment paper. Divide the dough into 4 equal pieces. With a rolling pin, on a sheet of parchment paper, roll out each piece into a rectangle that's about 4 in by 12 in [10 cm by 30.5 cm]. Use the paper to transfer the rectangles to the prepared sheet and refrigerate for 20 to 30 minutes.

Place the chilled rectangles in front of you with the longest sides nearest you. Using a small offset spatula, spread one-fourth of the fig jam in a thin strip horizontally across the center of each of the 4 rectangles. Fold the long sides of the dough over the jam, overlapping a bit, and pinching the dough closed with your fingers to form a seam. Remove the parchment from each rectangle and evenly place on the prepared baking sheet. Cover with plastic wrap, and refrigerate for 1 hour or for up to 3 days.

Preheat the oven to 350°F [180°C].

FOR THE EGG WASH Combine the egg and heavy cream in a small bowl.

Flip the dough rectangles over so the seam is on the bottom, brush the tops with the egg wash, and sprinkle with turbinado sugar. Bake 2 rectangles at a time on the prepared baking sheet, for about 20 minutes, rotating at the halfway point, until lightly browned. Cool to room temperature before cutting each rectangle into 12 equal pieces.

Store in an airtight container for up to 3 days.

№ **3**

Pies

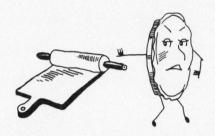

"THOUGH NO ONE REMEMBERS THE GENIUS WHO INVENTED THE PIE, NOBODY EVER FORGETS THE WOMAN WHO BAKES THE PERFECT ONE."

— McCall's Book of Cakes and Pies (1974)

VINTAGE ADVICE FOR THE MODERN KITCHEN

To prevent a pie with a soggy bottom crust, sprinkle a mixture of sugar and flour (or, my preference, a sprinkling of sugar and fine bread crumbs) on the unbaked crust before adding the filling.

BUTTERSCOTCH PIE WITH RUM–BLACK PEPPER WHIPPED CREAM

SERVES 8

Butterscotch pie just has an old-fashioned ring to it. The Butterscotch Pie from *Good Luck Desserts* (no date) is my inspiration here, though I topped mine with a rum–black pepper whipped cream, a flavor combo that has been a favorite of mine since testing the recipe for Triple Rum Black Pepper Bundt Cake from Matt Lewis and Renato Poliafito's second Baked cookbook, *Baked Elements*.

PIECRUST

1 cup plus 3 Tbsp [170 g] all-purpose flour

1½ tsp granulated sugar

¼ tsp baking powder

½ tsp salt

½ cup [110 g] unsalted butter, chilled

3 Tbsp ice water

1 tsp apple cider vinegar, chilled

EGG WASH

1 egg

Splash of heavy cream

FOR THE CRUST Combine the flour, granulated sugar, baking powder, and salt in the bowl of a food processer fitted with the metal blade and process briefly to combine. Cut the butter into cubes, add to the food processer, and pulse until the mixture resembles coarse meal.

Add the water and vinegar slowly, pulsing the machine only until the dough is crumbly, and a bit of dough can be pinched together between two fingers and hold its shape. Pour it into a bowl and, using your hands, shape the dough into a disk, wrap in plastic wrap, and refrigerate for at least 1 hour or up to 3 days.

Lightly flour a work surface and roll out the dough with a rolling pin until it is slightly wider than a 9-in [23-cm] deep-dish pie plate. Place the dough in the pie plate and decoratively crimp the edges. Using the tines of a fork, prick the bottom of the crust all over. Freeze for at least 1 hour.

Preheat the oven to 425°F [220°C].

BUTTERSCOTCH FILLING

1 cup [200 g] packed dark brown sugar

6 Tbsp [85 g] unsalted butter

1⅓ cups [320 ml] heavy cream, warmed

¼ cup [35 g] cornstarch

1¾ cups [420 ml] whole milk

2 egg yolks

1 egg

5 tsp pure vanilla extract

1½ tsp table salt

RUM–BLACK PEPPER WHIPPED CREAM

1½ cups [360 ml] heavy cream, chilled

¼ cup [30 g] confectioners' sugar

2 Tbsp dark rum

1 tsp freshly ground black pepper

Flaky sea salt for sprinkling

Line the piecrust with parchment paper and fill with pie weights (uncooked brown rice or dried beans).

FOR THE EGG WASH Combine the egg and cream in a small bowl and brush it on the crimped edges of the piecrust.

Bake the crust for 20 minutes, until the edges are brown and the bottom of the crust looks dry when you gently lift the parchment paper. Remove the paper and weights and return the crust to the oven until the bottom is nicely browned, about 10 minutes more. Set aside to cool.

FOR THE FILLING Combine the brown sugar and butter in a medium saucepan and carefully cook over medium to medium-high heat, stirring often with a wooden spoon, until the butter melts, the mixture boils, and it begins smelling caramel-like. Continue stirring for 3 minutes, lowering the heat to avoid burning, until the mixture is smooth and thickens. Remove from the heat, add the warm cream, and stir the caramel to combine.

In a large bowl, whisk together the cornstarch, milk, yolks, and egg. Return the caramel to medium to medium-high heat. Temper the egg mixture by adding spoonfuls of the warm caramel, one at a time, to the egg mixture, whisking constantly. Add all of the egg mixture to the warm caramel and whisk constantly until large bubbles begin popping on the surface. Continue to whisk for 45 to 60 seconds.

CONT'D

Remove from the heat. If it looks a bit lumpy, strain the filling through a wire mesh sieve into a large bowl. Add the vanilla and salt and whisk to combine. Transfer the filling to the cooled piecrust and refrigerate for at least 4 hours or overnight, tightly wrapped in plastic wrap.

FOR THE WHIPPED CREAM Place the cream in the bowl of a stand mixer fitted with the whisk attachment and whisk on medium to medium-high speed until the cream begins to thicken, 2 to 3 minutes. Add the confectioners' sugar, rum, and black pepper and continue whisking until medium peaks form.

To serve, sprinkle the pie with flaky sea salt, if using, and top each slice with a dollop of whipped cream. The pie will keep in the refrigerator, tightly wrapped in plastic wrap, for up to 3 days.

LEMON CHIFFON PIE WITH COCONUT WHIPPED CREAM

SERVES 8

Chiffon pies are fluffy and mousse-like with fillings that rely on gelatin, beaten egg whites, or whipped cream for their light-as-air texture. The lemon chiffon pie here borrows a little from two sources. It is just the right amount of sweet due to the recipe from *The Latest Cake Secrets* (1934). And it calls for folding beaten egg whites and lightly whipped cream into a lemon-gelatin base thanks to a recipe from *Aunt Chick's Pies* (1953). Then, I increased the lemon flavor of the filling by . . . A LOT, with more juice, zest, and lemon extract. I also call for rubbing the zest into the sugar with your fingers, which releases the zest's essential oils and results in more intense lemon flavor (thank you, Dorie Greenspan, for that tip).

SWEET TART DOUGH

1 cup [140 g]
all-purpose flour

½ cup [30 g] sweetened
shredded coconut

¼ cup [50 g]
granulated sugar

½ tsp table salt

6 Tbsp [85 g]
unsalted butter, at room
temperature

1 egg yolk,
lightly beaten

CONT'D

Grease a 9-in [23-cm] pie plate with nonstick cooking spray or softened butter and set aside.

FOR THE TART DOUGH Place the flour, coconut, granulated sugar, and salt in the bowl of a food processer fitted with the metal blade and process until combined. Cut the butter into small cubes, add to the bowl, and pulse until pea-size chunks form. Add the yolk and pulse until the dough begins to come together in clumps. It should hold together when you squeeze it between your fingers.

With your fingers, evenly press the dough into the bottom and sides of the pie plate. Using the tines of a fork, poke holes in the bottom of the piecrust all over. Freeze for at least 30 minutes or up to 3 days.

Preheat the oven to 375°F [190°C].

CONT'D

CHIFFON FILLING

½ envelope [1⅛ tsp] powdered gelatin

½ cup [100 g] granulated sugar

1 Tbsp grated lemon zest

2 eggs, separated

¼ tsp table salt

6 Tbsp [90 ml] freshly squeezed lemon juice

⅓ cup [80 ml] heavy cream, chilled

¼ tsp lemon extract

TOASTED COCONUT WHIPPED CREAM

⅔ cup [160 ml] heavy cream, chilled

2 Tbsp confectioners' sugar

¾ tsp coconut extract

¼ cup [15 g] sweetened shredded coconut, toasted (see page 168)

Press nonstick aluminum foil over the bottom and sides of the dough (do not cover the top edge of the crust in foil), forming a tight seal. Bake for 20 minutes, until the top edge of the crust is beginning to brown, and, when you lift the foil, the bottom no longer looks wet and shiny. Remove the foil, rotate the pan, and bake for 10 minutes more, until the crust is nicely browned. Let cool completely before filling.

FOR THE FILLING Add 2 tablespoons water to a small shallow bowl and sprinkle the gelatin over it. Let it bloom until the gelatin has been absorbed. Place half the granulated sugar and half the lemon zest in a small saucepan and rub the zest into the sugar with your fingers. Add the yolks and salt and whisk until combined. Add the lemon juice and whisk again.

Fill a large bowl with ice and have it ready near the stove top. Place the saucepan over medium heat and cook, without boiling, until the mixture thickens and coats the back of a spoon, about 5 minutes. Take the pan off the heat, add the bloomed gelatin, and whisk to combine. Pour into a medium bowl, set over the large bowl of ice, and let the mixture cool to room temperature, stirring occasionally.

Place the cream in the bowl of a stand mixer fitted with the whisk attachment and whisk on medium to medium-high speed until the cream begins to thicken, 2 to 3 minutes. Add the lemon extract and the remaining half of the lemon zest, and continue whisking until medium peaks form.

Add the whipped cream to the cooled filling and fold it in gently with a rubber spatula. Clean the mixer bowl and whisk attachment.

Add the egg whites to the clean mixer bowl, with a clean whisk attachment in place, and whisk on medium to medium-high speed until frothy. Add the remaining half of the granulated sugar in a slow and steady stream and continue to whisk until stiff, glossy peaks form, at least 5 minutes.

With a rubber spatula, gently fold the whites into the lemon filling in three installments. Transfer the filling to the pie plate, smooth the top, lightly cover with plastic wrap, and refrigerate for at least 4 hours until set, or overnight.

FOR THE WHIPPED CREAM Place the cream in the bowl of a stand mixer fitted with the whisk attachment and whisk on medium to medium-high speed until the cream begins to thicken, 2 to 3 minutes. Add the confectioners' sugar and coconut extract and continue whisking until medium peaks form. Fold in the toasted coconut (or save it to sprinkle on top).

Cover the lemon filling with the whipped cream and serve or refrigerate for up to 2 hours. The pie will keep lightly wrapped in plastic wrap in the refrigerator for up to 3 days.

PEANUT BUTTER CUSTARD PIE WITH MARSHMALLOW WHIPPED CREAM

SERVES 8

Baked custard pies were all the rage a century ago and remind me of what we call "pudding" or "cream" pies, save for the fact that a custard pie has no thickening agent and is baked. Here, I have fiddled with the Cup Custard recipe from *Baker's Pure Fruit Flavoring Extracts* (no date), by adding cornstarch and cooking it over the stove (as opposed to in the oven). I then added plenty of creamy peanut butter, kosher salt, and vanilla to ensure that this most flavorful—just this side of salty—peanut butter filling would be the perfect foil to the sweet, fluffy marshmallow whipped cream that crowns it.

1 Piecrust (pages 68–69), baked

PEANUT BUTTER CUSTARD

1½ cups [300 g] granulated sugar

5 Tbsp [50 g] cornstarch

1¼ tsp kosher salt

3 cups [720 ml] whole milk

1½ cups [360 ml] heavy cream

2 eggs, lightly beaten

¾ cup [195 g] creamy peanut butter (not all-natural)

1 Tbsp pure vanilla extract

FOR THE CUSTARD In a large saucepan, combine the sugar, cornstarch, and salt. Add the milk and cream and whisk. Add the eggs, whisk again, and place the saucepan over medium-high heat, whisking constantly.

Once the mixture begins to thicken and bubbles begin popping on the surface, decrease the heat to medium and whisk vigorously for 45 seconds to 1 minute. Remove the pan from the heat.

If the custard has any lumps, strain it through a wire mesh sieve into a heatproof bowl. Add the peanut butter and vanilla and whisk until incorporated. Let the custard cool briefly, and then transfer it to the pie shell and refrigerate until set, at least 4 hours, but preferably overnight, tightly wrapped in plastic wrap.

MARSHMALLOW WHIPPED CREAM

1½ cups [360 ml] heavy cream, chilled

2½ cups [250 g] marshmallow creme

Roasted salted peanuts for decorating

FOR THE WHIPPED CREAM Place the cream in the bowl of a stand mixer fitted with the whisk attachment and whisk on medium to medium-high speed until medium peaks form. With the mixer on low, add the marshmallow creme in two or three additions, whisking just until combined. Decoratively spread the whipped cream on the pie and sprinkle the top with salted roasted peanuts.

Serve immeditely or return to the refrigerator for up to 2 hours. The peanut butter pie will keep, lightly covered, in the refrigerator for up to 3 days.

MEXICAN HOT CHOCOLATE BAVARIAN PIE

SERVES 8

Piled high with billowy whipped cream or toasted meringue, nothing says 1950s diner dessert quite like chocolate pie. But even fifty years earlier, at the turn of the twentieth century, Chocolate Bavarian Cream, essentially chocolate pie filling with the addition of gelatin, was very popular. Here, I have modified a recipe from *Knox Gelatine Desserts, Salads, Candies and Frozen Dishes* (1936), adding Mexican hot chocolate spices to the filling and topping it with an ancho chile powder and black pepper toasted meringue. Marrying spicy and sweet flavors is a decidedly modern trend, and this pie is a perfect example of how well they pair.

CRUST

10 oz [280 g] vanilla wafers

2 Tbsp packed dark brown sugar

2 tsp ground cinnamon

½ tsp table salt

½ cup [110 g] unsalted butter, melted

FILLING

12 oz [340 g] semisweet chocolate, chopped

¼ cup [60 ml] whole milk

1 Tbsp powdered gelatin

2½ cups [600 ml] heavy cream

CONT'D

Preheat the oven to 350°F [180°C]. Grease a 9-in [23-cm] deep-dish pie plate with nonstick cooking spray or softened butter.

FOR THE CRUST In the bowl of a food processor fitted with the metal blade, process the wafers, brown sugar, cinnamon, and salt until combined. Add the melted butter and pulse until combined. Scrape down the bowl of the processor as needed.

Transfer the mixture to the prepared pie plate and, using your hands, press the mixture into the bottom of the plate and up the sides, creating a uniformly thick crust. Place the pie plate in the freezer for at least 30 minutes or up to 3 days, covered in plastic wrap.

Bake for 8 to 10 minutes, rotating at the halfway point, until the crust is lightly browned, fragrant, and dry to the touch. Let cool completely.

CONT'D

¼ cup [50 g]
granulated sugar

¾ tsp table salt

2 tsp ground cinnamon

½ tsp cayenne pepper,
or to taste

2 tsp pure vanilla extract

MERINGUE TOPPING

5 egg whites, at room
temperature

⅛ tsp table salt

¾ tsp pure vanilla extract

¼ tsp cream of tartar

⅛ tsp freshly ground
black pepper

¼ tsp ancho chile powder,
or to taste

1 cup [200 g]
granulated sugar

FOR THE FILLING Place the chocolate in a large bowl. Pour the milk into a small bowl and sprinkle the gelatin on top. Let it bloom until the gelatin has been absorbed.

In a medium saucepan, whisk together the cream, granulated sugar, salt, cinnamon, and cayenne. Place the saucepan over medium-high heat, whisking constantly. Once bubbles form on the surface, remove from the heat, add the bloomed gelatin, and whisk to combine. Pour the mixture over the chocolate and whisk until the chocolate melts. Whisk in the vanilla and pour the filling into the cooled pie shell until it is about ½ in [12 mm] below the edge of the crust. If you have extra filling, transfer it to a small bowl and refrigerate along with the pie—it is delicious on its own. Press plastic wrap on the surface of the filling to stop a skin from forming, and refrigerate for at least 4 hours until set, or overnight.

FOR THE MERINGUE In the bowl of a stand mixer fitted with the whisk attachment, add the egg whites, salt, vanilla, cream of tartar, black pepper, and chile powder and whisk together on medium speed until frothy. Add the granulated sugar in a slow and steady stream and continue to whisk on high speed until stiff, glossy peaks form, at least 5 to 7 minutes.

If you do not have a kitchen torch, preheat the broiler.

Spoon the meringue over the chilled pie, making sure the meringue touches the crust's edges.

Use the back of a spoon to make gentle swirls all over the top. Using a kitchen torch, toast the meringue topping, or toast the meringue in the oven for 1 to 2 minutes, watching closely to avoid burning. Refrigerate for at least 2 hours, lightly covered in plastic wrap.

The pie is best served the day it is made, but will keep in the refrigerator, lightly covered in plastic wrap, for up to 3 days.

LATTICED BLACKBERRY-LIME PIE

SERVES 8

It was the Blackberry Pie recipe from *What a Cook Ought to Know about Corn Starch* (1909) that inspired mine. I love the bare-bones filling instructions: "Wash blackberries, drain and fill plate quite full. Sprinkle well with sugar. Sift over all, one generous tablespoon . . . [cornstarch]." Done and done. I added lime juice and zest (for a little zing), a bit of butter atop my filling (for richness), and arrowroot powder instead of cornstarch (for a less cloudy filling), and tucked it all into a tender and flaky cream cheese crust.

CREAM CHEESE PIECRUST

2 cups plus 6 Tbsp [335 g] all-purpose flour

1 Tbsp granulated sugar

½ tsp baking powder

1 tsp salt

8 oz [230 g] cream cheese, chilled, cubed

1 cup [220 g] unsalted butter, chilled, cubed

1 Tbsp apple cider vinegar, chilled

1 Tbsp ice water

CONT'D

FOR THE CRUST Combine the flour, sugar, baking powder, and salt in the bowl of a food processer fitted with the metal blade and process briefly to combine. Add the cream cheese and butter, and pulse until the mixture resembles coarse meal.

Add the vinegar and ice water slowly, pulsing the machine as you do. Once a bit of dough can be pinched together between two fingers and hold its shape, dump it into a medium bowl and, using your hands, bring the dough together into 2 disks. Wrap each one in plastic wrap and refrigerate for at least 1 hour or up to 3 days.

Preheat the oven to 425°F [220°C]. Line a baking sheet with parchment paper.

Remove one disk from the refrigerator, lightly flour a work surface, and roll it into a 10- or 11-in [25- or 28-cm] circle. Place it in the pie plate and transfer to the refrigerator.

CONT'D

FILLING

1⅓ cups [265 g] granulated sugar

1 Tbsp grated lime zest

6 Tbsp [50 g] arrowroot powder

6 cups [720 g] fresh blackberries (do not use frozen)

2 tsp freshly squeezed lime juice

2 Tbsp unsalted butter

EGG WASH

1 egg

Splash of heavy cream

Turbinado sugar for sprinkling

Vanilla ice cream or lightly sweetened whipped cream (see page 169) for serving

FOR THE FILLING In a large bowl, combine the sugar and the zest and, using your fingers, rub the zest into the sugar. Add the arrowroot, the blackberries, and the lime juice. Toss with your hands to combine. Transfer the filling to the pie plate and dot the top with the butter.

Roll out the other half of dough into an 11-in [28-cm] circle. Using a pastry cutter or paring knife, cut the circle into 1-in [2.5-cm] strips. Transfer the strips to the prepared baking sheet, and, if your kitchen is warm, refrigerate briefly. If not, proceed with assembly.

Drape 6 or 7 strips of dough across the pie horizontally, leaving a little space between each one. Fold back every other strip halfway across the pie and place a strip across vertically at the halfway point. Fold the horizontal strips back over the vertical one. Fold back every other horizontal strip (different strips than you folded the last time), and place down another strip vertically. Continue doing so until you have latticed half the pie, and then do the other half. Trim the excess dough before decoratively crimping the edges.

FOR THE EGG WASH Combine the egg and cream in a small bowl, and brush it on the latticed dough. Sprinkle with turbinado sugar. Bake for 15 minutes, decrease the heat to 375°F [190°C], and bake for an additional 55 to 60 minutes, until the pie filling bubbles in the center of the pie. Tent the crust with aluminum foil after 30 minutes.

Let cool to room temperature, 4 hours, before serving with ice cream or whipped cream. The pie will keep loosely wrapped in plastic wrap on the counter for up to 3 days.

PUMPKIN-CHOCOLATE TART WITH CINNAMON WHIPPED CREAM

SERVES 8

Pumpkin pie is a classic, so it should come as no surprise that almost every vintage booklet includes a recipe for one. But, not with the addition of a chocolate cookie crust and a chocolate drizzle like this one! I tweaked the recipe from *The Rumford Modern Methods of Cooking* (1921), and added an extra egg and heavy cream instead of milk for a more luscious custard. The chocolate cookie crust is sublime with the pumpkin, both in color and taste, but if you're a purist, by all means use a traditional pastry dough (page 68).

CHOCOLATE COOKIE CRUMB CRUST

6 oz [170 g] crisp chocolate wafer cookies

1 Tbsp granulated sugar

5 Tbsp [75 g] unsalted butter, melted

PUMPKIN FILLING

1 cup [240 ml] heavy cream

2 eggs

1½ tsp pure vanilla extract

5 Tbsp [75 g] packed light brown sugar

3 Tbsp granulated sugar

10 oz [280 g] pumpkin purée

½ tsp table salt

CONT'D

Preheat the oven to 350°F [180°C].

FOR THE CRUST Place the wafers and granulated sugar in the bowl of a food processor fitted with the metal blade and process until finely ground. Add the melted butter and process until combined. Transfer the crumbs to a 9-in [23-cm] tart pan with a removable bottom and, using your fingers, press the crumbs evenly on the bottom of the pan and up the sides. Place the pan in the freezer for at least 30 minutes or up to 3 days, tightly covered in plastic wrap.

Bake the crust for 8 to 10 minutes, rotating at the halfway point, until dry to the touch and slightly puffy.

FOR THE FILLING In a large bowl, add the cream, eggs, and vanilla and whisk to combine. In a medium saucepan, combine the brown and granulated sugars, pumpkin purée, salt, cinnamon, ginger, and nutmeg and cook over medium heat, stirring constantly with

CONT'D

½ tsp ground cinnamon

½ tsp ground ginger

Rounded ¼ tsp
ground nutmeg

CHOCOLATE DRIZZLE

2 oz [55 g] dark chocolate,
melted (see page 169)

**CINNAMON WHIPPED
CREAM**

3 cups [720 ml] heavy
cream, chilled

½ cup [60 g] confectioners'
sugar, sifted

1 tsp pure vanilla extract

½ tsp ground cinnamon

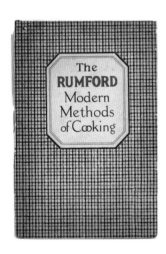

a wooden spoon, until the mixture bubbles and sputters. Continue to cook and stir the mixture for another 5 minutes.

Whisk the pumpkin mixture into the egg mixture, a little at a time so it does not curdle the eggs. If lumpy, strain the mixture through a wire mesh sieve, and transfer to the prepared tart pan. Do not fill the tart past the edge of the crust.

Bake for 20 to 25 minutes. Begin checking the tart at 15 minutes; it is ready when the center just jiggles the tiniest bit. Let cool completely on a wire rack on the counter before placing it in the refrigerator for at least 4 hours or up to overnight, tightly wrapped in plastic wrap.

FOR THE CHOCOLATE DRIZZLE Place the melted chocolate in a zippered plastic bag, cut a very tiny hole in the corner of the bag, and drizzle the chocolate over the tart. Let harden before serving.

FOR THE WHIPPED CREAM Place the cream in the bowl of a stand mixer fitted with the whisk attachment and whisk on medium to medium-high speed until the cream begins to thicken, 2 to 3 minutes. Add the confectioners' sugar, vanilla, and cinnamon and continue whisking until medium peaks form.

Serve slices of tart topped with a dollop of whipped cream.

The tart will keep, tightly covered in plastic wrap, in the refrigerator for up to 3 days.

CHERRY-ALMOND SLAB PIE WITH MARZIPAN CRUMBLE

SERVES 16

I have a special place in my heart for slab pie, which is traditionally baked in a rimmed baking sheet. It is for crust-lovers and those fond of Pop-Tarts. The recipe for Company Cherry Pie in *McCall's Book of Cakes and Pies* (1974) caught my eye and I modified the recipe, substituting a cherry filling from scratch for the canned cherries and red food coloring. I also added crumbles of almond paste and almond flour, as there is no more harmonious flavor combo.

ALMOND PIECRUST

2 cups [280 g]
all-purpose flour

¾ cup [90 g]
almond flour

⅓ cup [65 g]
granulated sugar

¾ tsp table salt

¾ cup [165 g] unsalted
butter, chilled

1 tsp almond extract

1 egg yolk

MARZIPAN CRUMBLE

1 cup [140 g]
all-purpose flour

7 oz [200 g] almond paste

CONT'D

Preheat the oven to 400°F [200°C].

Grease a 13-by-9-by-2-in [33-by-23-by-5-cm] pan with nonstick cooking spray or softened butter, line the bottom with parchment paper, and grease the paper.

FOR THE CRUST Combine the all-purpose and almond flours, the granulated sugar, and salt in the bowl of a food processor fitted with the metal blade and pulse to combine. Cut the butter into small cubes, add to the bowl, and pulse until coarse crumbs form. Add the almond extract, egg yolk, and ¼ cup [60 ml] cold water and continue to pulse until the dough begins to come together as a cohesive mass. Transfer the dough to the prepared pan and evenly press it into the bottom and two-thirds of the way up the sides of the pan. It will rip, but that is not a problem—simply press it back together again with your fingers. It may seem like there is not enough dough, but there is. Place in the freezer wrapped in plastic wrap while you assemble the filling and crumble, or for up to 3 days.

CONT'D

⅔ cup [130 g] granulated sugar

½ cup [110 g] unsalted butter, chilled

CHERRY FILLING

10 cups [1.3 kg] pitted cherries, fresh or frozen (do not thaw if frozen)

¾ cup [105 g] cornstarch

2 cups [400 g] granulated sugar

¼ tsp table salt

2 Tbsp freshly squeezed lemon juice

½ tsp almond extract

Sliced almonds for sprinkling

ALMOND GLAZE

1 cup [120 g] confectioners' sugar

¼ cup [60 ml] heavy cream

⅛ tsp almond extract

Vanilla ice cream for serving

FOR THE CRUMBLE In the same bowl of the food processor (no need to clean it), add the flour, almond paste, and granulated sugar and pulse to combine. Cut the butter into small cubes, add to the bowl, and process until a cohesive mass forms. Break the mass into crumbly bits, transfer to a bowl, cover with plastic wrap, and freeze until ready to use.

FOR THE FILLING Combine the cherries, cornstarch, granulated sugar, and salt in a large bowl and mix together. Add the lemon juice and almond extract and stir to combine.

To assemble the pie, place the filling in the crust and top with the crumble. Sprinkle a handful or two of sliced almonds on top.

Bake for 80 to 90 minutes, less time if you are using fresh cherries, rotating the pan after 30 minutes, and tenting the top with aluminum foil. The pie is ready when the filling is visibly bubbling and the center looks set. Let cool to room temperature before glazing.

FOR THE GLAZE Combine the confectioners' sugar, cream, and extract in a small bowl and whisk until smooth and glossy. Transfer the glaze to a zippered bag and cut a small hole in one corner. Squeezing gently, decorate the pie with the glaze. Let the glaze set, about 30 minutes, before serving with vanilla ice cream.

The pie will keep tightly covered in plastic wrap on the counter for up to 3 days.

STRAWBERRY-BASIL TURNOVERS

MAKES 8 LARGE TURNOVERS

I love a turnover: the extra crust, the portability, and the adorableness factor. The turnover recipe from *Secrets of the Jam Cupboard* (1930) influenced mine, although I substituted strawberry for the raspberry, and added plenty of fresh basil and black pepper to the berries. Like all turnovers, these are rustic—you fold the dough *over* the filling and pinch and seal with your fingers to bring it all together. A few tiny air vents allow a bit of bright red strawberry juice to leak out over the sparkly pastry while baking, which enhances their rustic charm.

2 Piecrusts (page 68)

FILLING

4 cups [455 g] strawberries, sliced

⅔ cup [130 g] granulated sugar

1½ Tbsp cornstarch

⅛ tsp table salt

¼ tsp freshly ground black pepper

1 Tbsp freshly squeezed lemon juice

⅔ cup [15 g] tightly packed fresh basil leaves, chopped

EGG WASH

1 egg

Splash of heavy cream

CONT'D

FOR THE FILLING In a small saucepan over medium-high heat, cook the strawberries, granulated sugar, cornstarch, salt, pepper, and lemon juice until sputtering, stirring frequently. Cook 5 minutes more, stirring constantly, until thickened. Bring to room temperature before adding the basil.

Line a baking sheet with parchment paper and set aside.

Remove the dough from the refrigerator and form 8 equal balls. Return 7 balls to the refrigerator and work with one ball at a time. Lightly flour a work surface and, with a rolling pin, roll out each ball, re-flouring as necessary, until it is about 7 in [17 cm] in diameter. Place the dough rounds on the prepared baking sheet, layering one on top of the other with small pieces of parchment paper between them. If your dough has softened, and you have trouble transferring the rounds to your sheet, return it to the refrigerator to chill briefly. Refrigerate the dough rounds for 10 minutes before assembling the turnovers.

CONT'D

Turbinado sugar for sprinkling

Vanilla ice cream for serving

FOR THE EGG WASH Combine the egg and the cream in a small bowl and whisk to combine.

For each turnover, brush half of the edge of the dough round with the egg wash. Spoon a rounded ¼ cup [45 g] filling onto the center of the rounds. Gently fold the dough over, forming a half-moon shape. Pinch the edges together to seal. Use a fork to decoratively mark the edge of the turnover. Using a paring knife, make 3 small slits in the top of the turnover. Repeat with the remaining dough. Remember: These turnovers are rustic looking and they *will* leak.

Transfer the turnovers on the baking sheet to the freezer for at least 1 hour, or overnight, tightly wrapped in plastic wrap. They will keep in the freezer for up to 3 days. Do not thaw before baking.

Preheat the oven to 425°F [220°C].

Brush the tops of the turnovers with egg wash and sprinkle with turbinado sugar. Bake for 25 to 30 minutes, rotating at the halfway point, or until the juices are bubbly and the crust is nicely browned.

Let cool for 15 minutes before serving with vanilla ice cream. Turnovers will keep on the counter, tightly covered in plastic wrap, for up to 3 days.

PEACH-GRAHAM CRACKER HAZELNUT CRISP

SERVES 12

To me, a peach crisp is the perfect comfort-food dessert. There is something so homey about the combination of peaches and graham crackers. After coming across Quick Peach Crisp in *Good Housekeeping's Book of Delectable Desserts* (1958), it wasn't long before I was crushing crackers, working in butter and sugar, and sprinkling it all over a baking dish full of fragrant sliced peaches. I altered the original recipe by using fresh peaches, not canned, sprinkling them with a bit of cinnamon, and adding toasted chopped hazelnuts to the topping for flavor and texture. Do not use packaged graham cracker crumbs in this recipe, and roughly crush the crackers to achieve the ideal texture; and leave the peach skins intact if you like; it adds a lovely color.

CRUMB MIXTURE

2 cups [240 g] crushed graham crackers, about 8 sheets

½ cup [110 g] unsalted butter, chilled and cut into cubes

½ cup [65 g] skinned hazelnuts, toasted and chopped (see page 168)

⅔ cup [130 g] packed light brown sugar

½ tsp pure vanilla extract

Preheat the oven to 350°F [180°C].

FOR THE CRUMB MIXTURE In a medium bowl, combine the graham crackers, butter, hazelnuts, brown sugar, and vanilla and, using your fingers, form small clumps of varying shapes. Place in the refrigerator.

FOR THE FILLING In a large bowl, combine the peaches, cornstarch, lemon juice, granulated sugar, and cinnamon and toss to combine.

Transfer the peaches to an 8-by-8-by-2-in [20-by-20-by-5-cm] baking pan, top with the graham cracker crumb mixture, and bake for 55 to 60 minutes, rotating at the halfway point and tenting with foil, until the topping is nicely browned and the filling is bubbling.

FILLING

2 lb [910 g] fresh peaches, sliced (do not use frozen)

3 Tbsp cornstarch

2 Tbsp freshly squeezed lemon juice

½ cup [100 g] granulated sugar

½ tsp ground cinnamon

Vanilla ice cream for serving

Let cool slightly before serving with ice cream.

The crisp will keep, tightly wrapped in plastic wrap, on the counter for up to 3 days.

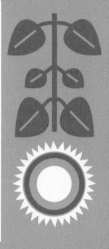

№ **4**

Cakes

"TO ALWAYS HAVE A PERFECT [CAKE] WITHOUT WORRY AND EFFORT IS EVERY WOMAN'S AMBITION."

— All About Home Baking (1940)

VINTAGE ADVICE FOR THE MODERN KITCHEN

Adding cold water to cake batter, rather than milk or buttermilk, as many recipes require, makes for the most tender of cakes.

DEVIL'S FOOD SHEET CAKE WITH SEA FOAM FROSTING

SERVES 16

Many of my booklets feature devil's food cake with sea foam frosting. Popularity aside, I'd have jumped at the chance to make anything topped with sea foam frosting, as the name alone is so enticing. I took the Rich Devil's Food Cake recipe from *11 Famous Recipes—Hershey's Cocoa* (1959) and turned it into a one-bowl chocolate cake—my favorite and super-easy to make. I used oil instead of shortening for moistness and added espresso powder to amp up the chocolate flavor. A generous sprinkling of sanding sugar in seaside colors enhances the beachy vibe.

DEVIL'S FOOD CAKE

1¾ cups [245 g]
all-purpose flour

¾ cup [60 g] Dutch-process
cocoa powder

1 cup [200 g] packed dark
brown sugar

1 cup [200 g]
granulated sugar

1 tsp baking soda

1¾ tsp baking powder

1 tsp table salt

1 egg

2 egg yolks

1 Tbsp pure vanilla extract

½ cup [120 ml] vegetable oil

CONT'D

Preheat the oven to 350°F [180°C]. Grease a 13-by-9-by-2-in [33-by-23-by-5-cm] pan with nonstick cooking spray or softened butter, line with parchment paper, and grease again.

FOR THE CAKE Add the flour, cocoa powder, brown sugar, granulated sugar, baking soda, baking powder, and salt to the bowl of a stand mixer fitted with the paddle attachment; mix on low speed until well combined.

In a small bowl, add the egg, egg yolks, vanilla, oil, and buttermilk and whisk until combined. With the mixer on medium-low speed, slowly pour the wet ingredients into the dry ingredients. Beat until incorporated, scraping down the bowl with a rubber spatula as needed.

In a small bowl, combine the boiling water and espresso powder and add to the batter in the mixer bowl. Mix again on medium speed for 30 seconds, until smooth. The batter will be quite thin.

CONT'D

1 cup [240 ml] buttermilk, at room temperature

1 cup [240 ml] boiling water

1 Tbsp espresso powder

SEA FOAM FROSTING

3 egg whites

1 cup plus 6 Tbsp [280 g] packed light brown sugar

1½ tsp light corn syrup

½ tsp cream of tartar

Dash of table salt

1 tsp pure vanilla extract

Blue and green sanding sugar for decorating

Pour the batter into the prepared pan and bake on the middle rack of the oven for 25 to 28 minutes, rotating at the halfway point. The cake is ready when a toothpick inserted in the middle comes out with a moist crumb or two. Let cool completely in the pan. The cake can be made 1 day ahead and kept tightly wrapped in plastic wrap on the counter.

FOR THE FROSTING Place a large heatproof bowl over a saucepan of simmering water over medium-high heat. Do not allow the bottom of the pan to touch the water. Add the egg whites, brown sugar, corn syrup, cream of tartar, salt, and 5 tablespoons [75 ml] water. Using an electric hand mixer, beat the egg white mixture on high speed until stiff and glossy, about 7 minutes. Remove the bowl from the saucepan of hot water, add the vanilla, and continue beating for another 2 minutes.

Generously frost the cake and sprinkle the top with sanding sugar. The frosted cake is best served within a few hours. The frosting dries and loses its "foamy" fluffiness pretty quickly but the cake can be kept, lightly covered, at room temperature for up to 3 days.

BLUEBERRY ANGEL FOOD DREAM

SERVES 16

I love angel food cake for its bright white, tight crumb and its very vanilla flavor. I also love that if you frost it with *brown sugar* whipped cream, you can call it "Angel Food Dream." The name is from *Learn to Bake . . . You'll Love It* (1947) and the recipe is from *The Swans Down Cake Manual* (1929). I decided to eliminate the almond extract and increase the amount of vanilla—my affection for deeply vanilla-flavored angel food cakes knows no bounds. I added blueberry compote to the whipped cream and sliced the cake in half to create more surface area on which to lavish the purple berry cream.

CAKE

1 cup [120 g] cake flour, sifted

1¼ cups [250 g] granulated sugar

¼ tsp table salt

12 egg whites, at room temperature

1¼ tsp cream of tartar

2 tsp pure vanilla extract

CONT'D

Preheat the oven to 350°F [180°C].

FOR THE CAKE In a medium bowl, sift together the flour, half of the sugar, and salt and set aside. Place the egg whites in the bowl of a stand mixer fitted with the whisk attachment and whisk on medium speed until foamy. Add 1 tablespoon water, the cream of tartar, and vanilla and whisk until just beginning to form soft peaks.

Add the remaining sugar, 1 tablespoon at a time, and whisk until incorporated. Continue whisking on medium speed until almost-stiff peaks form that are glossy and moist, and flop just a bit at the top when the whisk is raised. Sift the flour mixture over the whites, a little at a time, gently folding in the flour with each addition using a rubber spatula.

CONT'D

WHIPPED CREAM

2 cups [250 g] fresh or frozen blueberries, a handful reserved for garnish

⅓ cup [65 g] granulated sugar

2 cups [480 ml] heavy cream

¼ cup [50 g] packed light brown sugar

1½ tsp pure vanilla extract

Fresh blueberries for serving

Transfer the batter to an ungreased 10- to 12-cup [2.4- to 2.8-L] tube pan. Smooth the top with a small offset spatula or butter knife, and run the spatula through the batter to break up any air bubbles. Bake the cake for 35 to 40 minutes, rotating at the halfway point. The cake is ready when the top is browned and a cake tester comes out with a moist crumb or two. Place the pan upside-down on the neck of a wine bottle to cool completely. Using a small paring knife, release the cake from the sides of the pan and from the middle. Invert the cake right-side up onto a serving plate.

FOR THE WHIPPED CREAM Combine the blueberries, granulated sugar, and ½ cup [120 ml] water in a small saucepan and cook over medium to medium-high heat until the berries are loose and jammy, about 20 minutes. Let cool completely. If the mixture looks too thick once it has cooled, add 1 or 2 tablespoons of boiling water.

Place the cream in the bowl of a stand mixer fitted with the whisk attachment and whisk on medium to medium-high speed until the cream begins to thicken, 2 to 3 minutes. Add the brown sugar and vanilla and continue whisking until medium peaks form. Add the blueberry compote and whisk to combine.

Using a large serrated knife and a sawing motion, gently slice the cooled cake in half horizontally. Spread the whipped cream on the cut side of one cake layer, add the top layer, and spread the whipped cream all over the entire cake. Refrigerate for about 1 hour to set up.

Serve with a few fresh berries on each plate. The cake will keep refrigerated, lightly covered in plastic wrap, for up to 3 days.

CHOCOLATE-HAZELNUT MERINGUE CRADLE CAKE

SERVES 12

With its unusual assembly and even more unusual name, Meringue Cradle Cake is one of my favorites. You make a meringue with nuts and chocolate, create a "cradle" out of it, and fill it with cake batter. Genius. It's not surprising that the Meringue Cradle Cake was the third-place winner of the 1953 Pillsbury Bake-Off and then discovered by me among the pages of *Pillsbury's 4th Grand National 100 Prize Winning Recipes* (1953). The original was baked in a tube pan, but I use a loaf pan and slice it up like a teacake. This is not the prettiest of cakes, but it is one of the tastiest.

CAKE

1¼ cups [175 g] all-purpose flour

1¼ tsp baking powder

½ tsp table salt

¾ cup [180 ml] vegetable oil

¾ cup [150 g] granulated sugar

3 egg yolks

2 tsp pure vanilla extract

½ cup [120 ml] ice water

Preheat the oven to 325°F [165°C]. Grease a 9-by-5-by-3-in [23-by-12-by-7.5-cm] loaf pan with nonstick cooking spray or softened butter, line the bottom and the two short sides with one long piece of parchment paper, and grease the paper.

FOR THE CAKE In a small bowl, whisk together the flour, baking powder, and salt. In a medium bowl, add the oil and sugar and whisk to combine. In a small bowl, whisk together the yolks and vanilla.

Add the yolks and vanilla to the sugar-oil mixture and whisk vigorously to combine. Add half of the flour mixture, and gently fold with a rubber spatula to combine. Add the ice water, fold again, and fold in the remaining flour mixture until only a streak or two of flour remains.

MERINGUE

3 egg whites

¾ cup [150 g]
granulated sugar

¾ cup [70 g] hazelnut flour
(see page 168)

¾ oz [20 g] semisweet
chocolate, grated

Lightly sweetened whipped
cream (see page 169)
for serving

FOR THE MERINGUE In a stand mixer fitted with the whisk attachment, whisk the whites on medium speed until frothy. Add the sugar in a slow and steady stream and then continue to whisk on medium to medium-high speed until stiff, glossy peaks form. This will take at least 5 to 10 minutes. Gently fold the hazelnut flour and chocolate into the meringue with a rubber spatula. Transfer the meringue to the prepared loaf pan and, using a rubber spatula, spread it on the bottom and about two-thirds of the way up all four sides of the pan, leaving a 1½- to 2-in [4- to 5-cm] gap at the top, creating a cradle for the cake batter. Set aside.

Transfer the batter to the meringue cradle (it may rise above the edge) and bake for 55 to 65 minutes, rotating at the halfway point. It is done when a cake tester inserted into the center of the cake comes out with a moist crumb or two. Let the cake rest in the pan until cool enough to handle. Invert the cake, right-side up, onto a cooling rack, and let cool to room temperature before slicing.

The cake is delicious on its own or with a dollop of lightly sweetened whipped cream.

It will keep on the counter, tightly wrapped in plastic wrap, for up to 3 days.

CHOCOLATE-PEPPERMINT STICK ROLL

SERVS 12

My Party Book of Tested Chocolate Recipes (1938) includes a recipe for Chocolate Mint Roll that I was drawn to immediately, as Swiss rolls remind me of Drake's Yodels (a beloved childhood treat) and chocolate and mint is one of my favorite flavor combos. I love the simplicity of the *Party Book*'s recipe, but substituted a pink peppermint whipped cream with crushed candy canes for the original green seven-minute frosting (pink + candy canes + chocolate = dessert perfection), and a dark chocolate peppermint glaze instead of the "bittersweet coating," for a glossy, minty finish.

SPONGE CAKE

4 eggs, separated, at room temperature

⅓ cup [65 g] packed dark brown sugar

1½ tsp pure vanilla extract

3 Tbsp granulated sugar

Rounded ⅛ tsp table salt

Rounded ⅛ tsp cream of tartar

¼ cup [20 g] Dutch-process cocoa powder, plus extra for dusting

2 tsp espresso powder

1½ Tbsp boiling water

⅓ cup [40 g] cake flour

Rounded ½ tsp baking powder

Preheat the oven to 400°F [200°C]. Grease a 10-in-by-15-in [25-cm-by-38-cm] jelly roll pan with nonstick cooking spray or softened butter. Line the pan with parchment paper and grease again. Dust with cocoa powder, knocking out any excess, and set aside.

FOR THE CAKE Place the egg yolks in the bowl of a stand mixer fitted with the whisk attachment. Whisk the yolks on high speed, slowly adding the brown sugar, until thick and ribbony, at least 5 minutes. Add the vanilla and mix until incorporated.

Whisk the egg whites in a medium bowl, using a hand mixer on medium speed, until foamy. Slowly add the granulated sugar in a steady stream and continue whisking until soft peaks form. Add the salt and cream of tartar and whisk until stiff peaks form. With a rubber spatula, gently fold the whites into the yolks in three additions. Set aside.

Mix together 2 tablespoons of the cocoa powder, the espresso powder, and the boiling water in a small

DARK CHOCOLATE PEPPERMINT GANACHE

4 oz [115 g] dark chocolate, coarsely chopped

½ cup [120 ml] heavy cream

¼ tsp peppermint extract, or more to taste

FILLING

1½ cups [360 ml] heavy cream

3 Tbsp confectioners' sugar

3 to 4 Tbsp [45 to 60 ml] crème de menthe, optional

¾ tsp peppermint extract

2 or 3 drops red food coloring, optional

3 to 5 candy canes, crushed

bowl. Let cool to lukewarm. Fold it into the egg mixture with a rubber spatula.

Using a wire mesh sieve set over the egg mixture, sift the cake flour, the remaining 2 tablespoons cocoa powder, and the baking powder into the egg mixture. Gently fold the dry ingredients into the wet with a rubber spatula.

Gently spread the batter into the prepared pan, using an offset spatula or a butter knife. Bake for 5 to 7 minutes, until the cake just begins to pull away from the sides of the pan and a cake tester inserted in the center comes out clean.

Spread out a clean dish towel on the counter and sift cocoa powder over it and onto the top of the warm cake. Using a paring knife, release the cake from the edges of the pan. Invert the cake onto the cocoa-dusted dish towel and carefully remove the parchment paper from the cake. Sift additional cocoa powder over the cake. Cut about ¼ in [6 mm] off the edges of the cake all around and gently roll up the cake with the dish towel. Let the towel-wrapped cake rest on a cooling rack, seam-side down, until it reaches room temperature, at least 30 minutes.

FOR THE GANACHE Place the chocolate and cream in a small microwave-safe bowl and place in the microwave. Melt the chocolate on high power for 30 to 50 seconds, stirring the mixture every 10 seconds. Alternatively, set a small bowl with the chocolate and cream over a saucepan of simmering water and let the chocolate melt for 1 to 2 minutes, until smooth.

CONT'D

Stir in the peppermint extract and refrigerate for about 15 minutes to thicken a bit before using. This can be made up to 3 days ahead of time. Re-warm gently over a saucepan of simmering water before using, or in the microwave on high power, stirring every 15 seconds or so, until warm and pourable.

FOR THE FILLING Place the cream in the bowl of a stand mixer fitted with the whisk attachment and whisk on medium-high speed until the cream begins to thicken, 2 to 3 minutes. Add the confectioners' sugar, crème de menthe, if using, and peppermint extract, and continue whisking until medium peaks form. Add the food coloring, if using, to create a soft pink color, and whisk again just to incorporate.

Unroll the cooled cake and, using an offset spatula or butter knife, spread it with the filling, leaving a ¼-in [6-mm] border all around. Sprinkle with the crushed candy canes. Re-roll the cake without the towel, and transfer to a wire rack set over a baking sheet. Pour the ganache over the cake, and, using an offset spatula or butter knife, spread it over the roll. Refrigerate for at least 2 hours or overnight, lightly wrapped in plastic wrap. Transfer the cake to a serving plate and serve the cake straight from the refrigerator or let come to room temperature. Slice it with a large serrated knife.

Serve with a sprinkling of crushed candy canes. The cake will keep in the refrigerator, lightly wrapped in plastic wrap, for up to 3 days.

SILVER CAKE WITH PINK FROSTING

SERVES 16

This early to mid-twentieth-century white cake is made with nary an egg yolk but with copious amounts of stiffly peaked egg whites. I encountered many recipes for this cake, often with slight variations on the name—Silver Sea Foam Loaf, Penny-Wise Silver Cake, and Silver White Cake. I revamped a recipe for White Moon Cake from *Home Baked Delicacies* (1931) and I substituted ice water for the milk as ice water makes for the most tender of cake crumbs. I frosted the cake in pink buttercream and sprinkled the whole thing with sanding sugar.

CAKE

2¼ cups [270 g] cake flour, sifted

2 tsp baking powder

½ tsp baking soda

1 tsp table salt

½ cup [90 g] vegetable shortening

¼ cup [55 g] unsalted butter, at room temperature

2 tsp pure vanilla extract

1½ cups [300 g] granulated sugar

1 cup [240 ml] ice water

4 egg whites, stiffly beaten (see page 169)

CONT'D

Preheat the oven to 350°F [180°C]. Grease two 9-in-by-2-in [23-cm-by-5-cm] round cake pans with non-stick cooking spray or softened butter. Line with parchment paper and grease again.

FOR THE CAKE In a medium bowl, whisk together the flour, baking powder, baking soda, and salt. In the bowl of a stand mixer fitted with the paddle attachment, beat the shortening, butter, and vanilla on medium to medium-high speed until fluffy and light, 2 to 3 minutes, scraping down the bowl with a rubber spatula as needed. Add the granulated sugar and continue beating for another 3 to 5 minutes, until the mixture doubles in volume.

Decrease the speed to low and add the dry ingredients in three additions, alternating with two additions of the water, scraping down the bowl as needed with a rubber spatula. Stop the mixer when there are still streaks of flour in the batter. Finish mixing by hand, adding the egg whites in three stages, and folding them in with a rubber spatula.

CONT'D

PINK BUTTERCREAM

1½ cups [330 g] unsalted butter, at room temperature

½ tsp table salt

6 cups [720 g] confectioners' sugar, sifted

⅔ cup [160 ml] whole milk or heavy cream

4 tsp pure vanilla extract

Red food coloring, optional (but so pretty)

Pink sanding sugar for decorating

HOME BAKED DELICACIES

new edition!

ENHANCE THE FAME OF THE MODERN HOSTESS

Transfer the batter to the prepared pans and bake for 20 to 25 minutes, rotating at the halfway point. The cakes are ready when a cake tester comes out with a few moist crumbs and the cake has just started to come away from the sides of the pan. Let cool for about 20 minutes, and invert the cakes right-side up onto cooling racks. Let the cakes cool to room temperature. The cakes can be tightly wrapped in plastic wrap and stored on the counter for up to 1 day.

FOR THE BUTTERCREAM In the cleaned bowl of the stand mixer fitted with the paddle attachment, beat the butter on medium speed until smooth and soft. On low speed slowly add the salt and 2 cups [240 g] of the confectioners' sugar, scraping the bowl periodically with a rubber spatula. Add one-fourth of the milk and mix until incorporated. Continue mixing in this manner, adding the remaining confectioners' sugar and milk, until the frosting is fluffy and spreadable.

Add the vanilla and a few drops of food coloring, if using, and continue mixing on medium-low to medium speed for at least 5 minutes, until fluffy and stable. A longer mixing time results in exceptionally light frosting. The frosting will keep on the counter in an airtight container for up to 1 day, but may need to be re-whipped in a stand mixer before using.

Generously frost the cooled cake layers with the buttercream, using an offset spatula or butter knife. If you do not want a thickly frosted cake, you will have leftover frosting. Sprinkle sanding sugar on top of the first frosted layer, before placing the second on top of it, and on the top and sides of the frosted cake once you are done. Slice the cake using a long serrated knife. The cake will keep, lightly covered in plastic wrap, on the counter for up to 3 days.

COCONUT BLITZ TORTE

SERVES 12

Allow me to introduce you to the blitz torte: a two-layer cake in which cake batter is covered in glossy, soft meringue, and baked. Once cooled, the meringue-coated layers are placed atop each other with a layer of whipped cream (or fruit filling) sandwiched between them. I took the blitz torte recipe from *Cake Secrets* (1953) and gave it a modern makeover via coconut in all its forms. Shredded coconut goes into the cake batter, coconut oil replaces some of the shortening, coconut milk is used instead of regular milk, and a coconut whipped cream filling is swapped for the pineapple one. Yes, coconut lovers, I've got your back.

CAKE

1½ cups [210 g]
all-purpose flour

1½ tsp baking powder

¼ tsp baking soda

½ tsp table salt

½ cup [110 g] unsalted
butter, at room temperature

¼ cup [60 ml] coconut or
vegetable oil

1⅓ cups [265 g]
granulated sugar

1 Tbsp pure vanilla extract

5 egg yolks, at
room temperature

CONT'D

Preheat the oven to 350°F [180°C]. Remove the top oven rack, as the meringue rises quite a bit while baking. Generously grease two 8-by-8-by-2-in [20-by-20-by-5-cm] cake pans with nonstick cooking spray or softened butter. Line the bottom of the pans with parchment paper and grease again.

FOR THE CAKE In a medium bowl, add the flour, baking powder, baking soda, and salt and whisk together. In the bowl of a stand mixer fitted with the paddle attachment, beat the butter on medium to medium-high speed until fluffy and light, 2 to 3 minutes, scraping down the bowl with a rubber spatula as needed. Add the coconut oil, granulated sugar, and vanilla and continue beating for another 3 to 5 minutes, until the mixture at least doubles in volume.

CONT'D

¾ cup [180 ml] full-fat coconut milk, at room temperature

¾ cup [45 g] lightly packed shredded sweetened coconut

MERINGUE

5 egg whites, at room temperature

¼ tsp cream of tartar

1 cup [200 g] granulated sugar

1 cup [60 g] lightly packed shredded sweetened coconut

WHIPPED CREAM

1½ cups [360 ml] heavy cream

¼ cup [30 g] confectioners' sugar

1 tsp coconut extract, or to taste

Decrease the speed to low and add the yolks, one at a time, scraping the bowl after each addition. Add the dry ingredients in three additions, alternating with two additions of the coconut milk, scraping the bowl as needed with a rubber spatula. Stop the mixer and remove the bowl when there are still streaks of flour in the batter. Finish mixing by hand.

Fold in the coconut and transfer the batter to the prepared pans. Using a small offset spatula or butter knife, smooth the tops of the layers and set them aside while you make the meringue.

FOR THE MERINGUE Clean the bowl of the mixer and the whisk attachment. Place the egg whites in the cleaned mixer bowl with the cream of tartar, and whisk on medium speed until frothy. Add the granulated sugar in a slow and steady stream and continue to whisk the whites on medium-high speed, until glossy, soft peaks form. This will take up to 5 minutes or more. Divide the meringue between the two cake pans and smooth the meringue over the cake layers with a small offset spatula or a butter knife.

Bake for 35 to 40 minutes, rotating and sprinkling the coconut over each layer at the halfway point. The cake is ready when a tester inserted in the center comes out with a few moist crumbs and the meringue topping has risen considerably and is lightly browned, billowy, and crackly. Don't be afraid to poke your meringue with the tester when checking on the doneness of the cake. It will deflate, but will do so anyway when you remove the cake from the oven.

Let the cakes cool completely on a wire rack before removing them from the pans, running a paring knife around the edge to release the meringue before doing so. Carefully invert them onto cooling racks and then immediately flip them back over so the meringue is on top.

FOR THE WHIPPED CREAM Place the cream in the bowl of a stand mixer fitted with the whisk attachment and whisk on medium to medium-high speed until the cream begins to thicken, 2 to 3 minutes. Add the confectioners' sugar and coconut extract and continue whisking until medium peaks form.

Place one cake layer on a serving dish. Spread all of the whipped cream on top of it, using an offset spatula or butter knife. Place the second layer on top and press down lightly on the top of the cake.

Serve immediately, or let the cake sit at room temperature for up to 1 hour. The cake is best the day it is made, but will keep, lightly wrapped in plastic wrap, in the refrigerator for up to 3 days.

CARAMEL-FILLED BANANA CUPCAKES WITH PENUCHE FROSTING

MAKES 36 CUPCAKES

I think it's fair to say that housewives went a little "bananas" for banana cake during the first half of the twentieth century. The recipe revamped here is from *20 Wonderful Cakes made by the new Kraft Oil Method* (1955). I increased the amount of bananas and frosted these with penuche, a brown sugar-based frosting with an almost caramel-like flavor. And the salty caramel filling? Well, not only does salty caramel rank almost with bacon on the trendy scale these days, but it beautifully marries the flavor of the penuche to the bananas.

SALTY CARAMEL

½ cup [160 g] light
corn syrup

1 cup [200 g]
granulated sugar

¾ cup [180 ml]
heavy cream, warmed

3 Tbsp unsalted butter

2 tsp pure vanilla extract

½ tsp table salt

CUPCAKES

3 cups [360 g] cake flour,
sifted

1 tsp baking soda

1 tsp baking powder

½ tsp table salt

FOR THE SALTY CARAMEL In a deep medium saucepan, using a wooden spoon, stir the corn syrup, granulated sugar, and ⅓ cup [80 ml] water together until combined. Place the saucepan over medium heat until the sugar dissolves. Increase the heat to medium-high, and cook the sugar mixture until it colors to deep amber, 12 to 15 minutes. Do not stir the mixture, but, holding the pan handles, gently swirl the mixture to ensure the sugar cooks evenly and that the color is to your liking (the deeper the color, the stronger the flavor of the caramel).

Decrease the heat, and carefully pour in the heavy cream, as the mixture will bubble up. Stir with a wooden spoon until any and all bits of hardened caramel melt. Remove the pan from the heat and add the butter, vanilla, and salt, stirring until everything is incorporated.

Let the caramel cool to room temperature before using. The caramel can be made up to 1 week ahead and refrigerated in an airtight container. Bring to

½ cup [110 g] unsalted butter, at room temperature

⅓ cup [80 ml] vegetable oil

1¼ cups [250 g] packed light brown sugar

¾ cup [150 g] granulated sugar

2 eggs

1 egg yolk

1 Tbsp pure vanilla extract

4 ripe bananas, mashed

¾ cup [180 g] sour cream

PENUCHE FROSTING

1 cup [220 g] unsalted butter

2 cups [400 g] packed light brown sugar

½ cup [120 ml] heavy cream

4 cups [480 g] confectioners' sugar, sifted

2 tsp pure vanilla extract

1 tsp table salt

Flaky sea salt for sprinkling

room temperature, however, before filling the cups, which is done prior to making the penuche frosting.

Preheat the oven to 350°F [180°C]. Fill three 12-cup muffin tins with cupcake liners and set aside.

FOR THE CUPCAKES In a medium bowl, Whisk together the flour, baking soda, baking powder, and salt. In the bowl of a stand mixer fitted with the paddle attachment, beat the butter on medium to medium-high speed until fluffy and light, 2 to 3 minutes, scraping down the bowl with a rubber spatula as needed. Add the oil, brown sugar, and granulated sugar and continue beating for another 3 to 5 minutes, until the mixture at least doubles in volume.

Decrease the speed to low and add the eggs and the yolk, one at a time, beating well and scraping the bowl with a rubber spatula after each addition. Add the vanilla and the bananas, and scrape down the bowl. Add the dry ingredients in three additions, alternating with two additions of sour cream, scraping the bowl as needed. Stop the mixer when there are still streaks of flour in the batter and finish mixing by hand.

Fill each cup two-thirds full, and bake for 20 to 22 minutes, rotating the pan at the halfway point. These cook for slightly longer than a regular cupcake, as they need to be extra sturdy once filled. The cupcakes are ready when a cake tester comes out clean and the tops are nicely browned. Let them cool in the pan for 10 minutes and transfer the cupcakes to a wire rack to cool to room temperature. The cupcakes can be filled immediately, or they can be tightly covered in plastic wrap and left on the counter for up to 1 day.

CONT'D

To fill the cupcakes, press the small end of a large frosting tip into the center of the top of each cupcake. Twist the tip as you pull it out to remove the center of the cupcake, leaving a cavity for the caramel. You can also use a small paring knife to cut a narrow, deep hole into the center of each cup.

If the caramel is too thick, warm it gently in a small saucepan over low heat, or in the microwave on high power in 10-second bursts, until just pourable. Using a small spoon, place a spoonful or two of the caramel into the hole on the top of each cupcake. Alternatively, you can fill a zippered plastic bag with the caramel and cut a small piece off the corner. Squeeze the bag to inject a little caramel into the hole. Wait until the caramel is fully absorbed and add more until the cavity is filled. Set the filled cupcakes aside.

FOR THE PENUCHE FROSTING Combine the butter, brown sugar, and cream in a medium saucepan over medium-high heat, and bring to a boil, stirring occasionally. Let simmer for about 2 minutes, stirring constantly. Remove from the heat and let cool slightly. Add the confectioners' sugar, vanilla, and salt and whisk vigorously until thick and spreadable, 3 to 5 minutes.

Spread the frosting on each cupcake using a small offset spatula, butter knife, or the back of a spoon. If the frosting becomes difficult to spread, whisk in a few drops of hot water until it becomes spreadable again. Sprinkle with flaky sea salt.

The cupcakes will keep, lightly covered in plastic wrap, on the counter for up to 3 days.

RASPBERRY-MARSHMALLOW UPSIDE-DOWN CAKE

SERVES 12

The book *250 Classic Cake Recipes* (1954) includes an entire section on upside-down cakes—everything from apple gingerbread to fruit mélange. Then I found one calling for rhubarb and *marshmallows*! I loved the crazy-sounding combo of fruit and marshmallows (the marshies caramelize around the fruit in the bottom of the pan in the most delicious of ways). My recipe replaces the rhubarb with raspberries, and I added more marshmallows than called for in the original (because marshmallows + caramelized = heaven). If you also want to sprinkle a few on top of the cake prior to baking, I'm right there with you.

1⅓ cups [185 g]
all-purpose flour

1½ tsp baking powder

¼ tsp table salt

1 cup [200 g]
granulated sugar

½ cup [120 ml] vegetable oil

2 tsp pure vanilla extract

1 egg

1 egg yolk

½ cup [120 ml] buttermilk,
at room temperature

2 cups [240 g] fresh
or frozen raspberries
(do not thaw if frozen)

Preheat the oven to 350°F [180°C]. Grease an 8-by-8-by-2-in [20-by-20-by-5-cm] square pan with non-stick cooking spray or softened butter. Set aside.

In a medium bowl, whisk together the flour, baking powder, and salt. In a large bowl, vigorously whisk together the granulated sugar, oil, and vanilla until well combined. Add the egg and yolk and whisk again. Add the buttermilk and whisk again.

Add the dry ingredients to the wet and, using a rubber spatula, gently fold together until no streaks of flour remain.

Combine the raspberries, marshmallows, and brown sugar in a medium bowl, stir together, and place in the bottom of the prepared pan. Transfer the cake batter to the pan, covering the berries and marshmallows, and spreading it with a small offset spatula if necessary. Sprinkle the top with a few extra marshmallows, if using.

Generous 1½ cups [75 g]
mini marshmallows, plus
more for sprinkling,
optional

¼ cup [50 g] packed light
brown sugar

Confectioners' sugar
for dusting

Heavy cream for dribbling

Bake for about 50 minutes, rotating the pan at the halfway point. Begin to check on the cake with a cake tester after about 40 minutes. The cake is done when it is lightly browned, is just beginning to come away from the sides of the pan, and a tester comes out clean or with a moist crumb or two.

Let the cake cool briefly on a wire rack.

Serve slices warm, directly from the pan, using a serving spoon to scoop out the pieces. Flip the pieces over on the serving plates so that the fruit is facing up. Dust with confectioners' sugar and dribble with heavy cream (a necessity, if you ask me).

The cake will keep, tightly covered in plastic wrap, for a few days on the counter, but is best served warm the day it is made.

"S'MORE" GRAHAM CRACKER CAKE

SERVES 12

I was pretty excited when I discovered that graham cracker cake was a common early- to- mid-century treat because such a cake immediately brings s'mores to my twenty-first-century mind. Here, I've taken the recipe for Chocolate Graham Cracker Cake from *Hershey's Favorite Recipes* (1937) and filled it with a whipped milk chocolate ganache. Be warned: This is not your typical cake but something more complex, less sweet, and almost earthy. The cake layers are actually made of crushed graham crackers—and truly taste of them. To top it all off is the fluffiest toasted marshmallow frosting you ever did see.

MILK CHOCOLATE GANACHE

7 oz [200 g] milk chocolate, coarsely chopped

¼ tsp table salt

½ cup [120 ml] heavy cream

CAKE

2 cups [280 g] all-purpose flour

1½ cups [180 g] graham cracker crumbs

2¼ tsp baking powder

¼ tsp baking soda

¾ tsp table salt

1 cup plus 3 Tbsp [265 g] unsalted butter, at room temperature

FOR THE GANACHE Place the chocolate and salt in a small heatproof bowl. Heat the cream in a small saucepan over medium heat, or in the microwave on high power, in 10-second bursts, until small bubbles appear on the surface. Pour the hot cream over the chocolate and let sit for 1 minute. Mix the chocolate and cream together until completely combined. Let sit for at least 1 hour until the ganache thickens to a spreadable consistency.

Preheat the oven to 350°F [180°C]. Grease two 9-in-by-2-in [23-cm-by-5-cm] round cake pans with nonstick cooking spray or softened butter. Line with parchment paper, grease again, and set aside.

FOR THE CAKE In a medium bowl, whisk together the flour, cracker crumbs, baking powder, baking soda, and salt. In the bowl of a stand mixer fitted with the paddle attachment, beat the butter, on medium to medium-high speed, until fluffy and light, 2 to 3 minutes, scraping down the bowl with a rubber spatula as needed. Add the sugars and continue beating for another 3 to 5 minutes, until the mixture at least doubles in volume. Decrease the speed to low, add the eggs and yolks, one at a time, and then

1 cup [200 g] packed light brown sugar

¾ cup [150 g] granulated sugar

2 eggs

3 egg yolks

2¼ tsp pure vanilla extract

1 cup plus 3 Tbsp [285 ml] whole milk

MARSHMALLOW FROSTING

5 egg whites

1¾ cups [350 g] granulated sugar

2¼ tsp light corn syrup

½ tsp cream of tartar

¼ tsp table salt

1 tsp pure vanilla extract

the vanilla. Add the dry ingredients in three additions, alternating with two additions of the milk. Stop the mixer when there are still streaks of flour in the batter. Finish mixing by hand.

Transfer the batter to the prepared pans and bake for 24 to 26 minutes, rotating at the halfway point. The cakes are ready when a cake tester comes out with a moist crumb and the cake has just started to pull away from the sides of the pan. Let cool for 10 minutes and invert the cakes onto a wire rack. Let cool to room temperature.

Place the ganache in a stand mixer fitted with the whisk attachment and whisk on medium-high speed until light in color and fluffy, 2 to 3 minutes. Spread it on one of the cake layers with an offset spatula or butter knife; do not top with the other layer yet.

FOR THE FROSTING Place the egg whites, sugar, ½ cup [120 ml] water, corn syrup, cream of tartar, and salt in a large heatproof bowl. Set the bowl on top of a saucepan of boiling water over medium-high heat (do not let the water touch the bottom of the bowl). Using an electric hand mixer on high speed, beat the egg white mixture until stiff and glossy, about 7 minutes. Remove the bowl, add the vanilla, and beat for 1 to 2 minutes.

Spread a layer of frosting on top of the cake layer with the ganache. Top with the other cake layer. Frost the cake generously. Use a kitchen torch, if you have one, to toast the marshmallow. Use a long serrated knife to slice the cake and serve immediately.

The cake can be kept, lightly covered in plastic wrap, on the counter for up to 3 days, but is best the day it is made.

STRAWBERRY SHORTCAKE

SERVES 8

When I think of strawberry shortcake, slightly sweetened biscuits filled with berries and cream come to mind. Diners get their own individual dessert and are the happier for it, as individual desserts do that to people. However, back in the day, shortcakes were often made in round 8-in [20-cm] cake pans. Here, I have toyed with just such a shortcake—referred to as a Fruit Fantasy in *Some of My Favorite Good Things to Eat* (1940). I baked it in one pan and sliced it into two layers before filling it with fresh fruit, as opposed to the canned option offered in the original (you're welcome).

STRAWBERRY FILLING

4 cups [455 g] strawberries, hulled and sliced

¼ cup [50 g] granulated sugar

SHORTCAKE

2 cups [280 g] all-purpose flour

1 cup [120 g] cake flour

5 Tbsp [75 g] granulated sugar

1 Tbsp baking powder

⅛ tsp baking soda

1 tsp table salt

¾ cup [165] unsalted butter, chilled

1 cup [240 ml] heavy cream

Preheat the oven to 425°F [220°C]. Line an 8-in-by-2-in [20-cm-by-5-cm] round pan with parchment paper and set aside.

FOR THE STRAWBERRY FILLING Combine the berries and granulated sugar in a medium bowl and allow to macerate on the counter while you prepare and bake the shortcake.

FOR THE SHORTCAKE Add the all-purpose and cake flours, sugar, baking powder, baking soda, and salt to the bowl of a food processor fitted with the metal blade. Cut the butter into small cubes, add to the bowl, and pulse until the mixture resembles coarse meal. Dump the mixture into a large bowl and add the heavy cream. Using a wooden spoon, combine the wet ingredients into the dry, until a shaggy dough forms.

Dump the dough out onto the counter. Knead the dough until it just comes together and gently press it into the prepared pan. The dough will be crumbly.

EGG WASH

1 egg

Splash of heavy cream

Turbinado sugar for
sprinkling

WHIPPED CREAM

1½ cups [360 ml]
heavy cream

¼ cup [30 g]
confectioners' sugar

1 tsp pure vanilla extract

FOR THE EGG WASH Combine the egg and heavy cream in a small bowl and brush the egg wash on the top of the shortcake. Sprinkle with the turbinado sugar.

Bake for 5 minutes. Decrease the heat to 400°F [200°C] and bake for 18 to 22 minutes, rotating the pan at the halfway point. The shortcake is ready when it is golden brown and a cake tester inserted in the center comes out clean. If the top browns too much before the cake is fully baked, tent it with aluminum foil.

Place the pan on a cooling rack for about 15 minutes, until cool enough to handle. Invert the cake onto a serving plate, so it is right-side up, and let it come almost to room temperature.

FOR THE WHIPPED CREAM Place the cream in the bowl of a stand mixer fitted with the whisk attachment and whisk on medium to medium-high speed until the cream begins to thicken, 2 to 3 minutes. Add the confectioners' sugar and vanilla and continue whisking until medium peaks form.

Slice the cake in half horizontally with a large serrated knife. Place strawberries and their juice on the bottom layer, and place the top layer over the berries.

Slice and serve with a generous dollop of whipped cream. The cake is best eaten the day it is made.

COTTAGE PUDDING WITH VANILLA SAUCE

SERVES 12

Cottage pudding is not pudding at all, but a simple yellow cake, baked in a square pan, and served with sauce, be it vanilla, chocolate, butterscotch, lemon, nutmeg, or even rhubarb. I consider it the perfect snack cake. I started with the recipe from *Davis Cook Book: The Pure Food Kind* (no date) and added an egg yolk, and a tad more butter and sugar, and I substituted buttermilk for the milk to make it more moist, flavorful, and tender. For the sauce I used heavy cream instead of water for richness and cornstarch instead of flour for efficiency (it thickens more quickly than flour does).

COTTAGE PUDDING

2¼ cups [270 g] cake flour, sifted

1¼ tsp baking powder

¼ tsp baking soda

1 tsp table salt

1 cup [220 g] unsalted butter, at room temperature

1¾ cups [350 g] granulated sugar

1 Tbsp pure vanilla extract

2 eggs

1 egg yolk

1 cup [240 ml] buttermilk

Preheat the oven to 350°F [180°C]. Grease an 8-by-8-by-2-in [20-by-20-by-5-cm] square pan with nonstick cooking spray or softened butter, line with parchment paper, and grease again.

FOR THE PUDDING In a medium bowl, whisk together the flour, baking powder, baking soda, and salt. In the bowl of a stand mixer fitted with the paddle attachment, beat the butter on medium-high speed until fluffy and light, 2 to 3 minutes, scraping down the bowl with a rubber spatula as needed. Add the granulated sugar and vanilla and continue beating for another 3 to 5 minutes, until the mixture at least doubles in volume.

Decrease the speed to low and add the eggs and yolk, one at a time, scraping the bowl after each addition. Add the dry ingredients in three additions, alternating with two additions of the buttermilk, scraping the bowl as needed with a rubber spatula. Stop the mixer and remove the bowl when there are still streaks of flour in the batter. Finish mixing by hand.

VANILLA SAUCE

½ cup [60 g] confectioners'
sugar, sifted

1 Tbsp cornstarch

1 cup [240 ml] heavy cream

2 Tbsp unsalted butter

1 Tbsp pure vanilla extract

⅛ tsp table salt

Lightly sweetened whipped
cream for serving, optional
(see page 169)

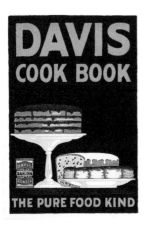

Slowly transfer the batter to the prepared pan (it will be very full) and bake for 35 to 45 minutes, mindfully rotating the cake at the halfway point. The cake is ready when a cake tester inserted in the center comes out with a moist crumb or two and the cake has just started to come away from the sides of the pan. If the edges get too brown before the cake is ready to be pulled from the oven, tent it with aluminum foil. Let it cool for 10 minutes. Invert the cake onto a cooling rack, so it is right-side up, and let come to room temperature.

FOR THE SAUCE Whisk together the confectioners' sugar and cornstarch in a small bowl. Warm the cream over medium heat in a small saucepan. Once bubbles appear around the perimeter of the cream, add the sugar-cornstarch mixture and stir with a wooden spoon until thickened, 3 to 5 minutes. Add the butter, vanilla, and salt and whisk to combine.

Transfer the cake to a serving plate and serve sliced and dribbled with the sauce and a dollop of whipped cream on the side if you like. The cake will keep, tightly wrapped in plastic wrap, on the counter for up to 3 days. The sauce can be refrigerated in an airtight container for up to 3 days. Reheat it in a microwave on high power for 30 to 60 seconds, or on the stove top over medium heat until warm, before serving.

$N\!\underline{o}$

5

Refrigerator Desserts

"FIRST AID TO THE HARRIED HOSTESS IS... REFRIGERATOR CAKE PREPARED AHEAD OF TIME."

– 250 Luscious Refrigerator Desserts (1954)

VINTAGE ADVICE FOR THE MODERN KITCHEN

Whip cream only to a soft peak prior to adding it to a refrigerator pie or other chilly treat. If the cream is whipped too stiffly, it will lack volume and have a "buttery" flavor after refrigeration.

STRAWBERRY-LEMON CHARLOTTE RUSSE WITH THYME LADYFINGERS

SERVES 16

A Charlotte Russe, made by layering sponge cake, ladyfingers, or cookies with a creamy filling, and often stabilized with gelatin, is akin to a trifle or an icebox cake. The one updated here from the *New Royal Cook Book* (1922) is simplicity itself: "Sponge cake or lady fingers . . . to be fill[ed] with whipped cream and serve[d] cold." I unpacked the instructions a bit, and have called for homemade thyme ladyfingers and a boozy filling of lemon whipped cream and strawberries. Mid-century housewives often used store-bought ladyfingers for their Russes and you can, too—just add a teaspoon or two of thyme to your whipped cream.

LADYFINGERS

4 eggs, separated

7 Tbsp [105 g] granulated sugar

1½ tsp pure vanilla extract

⅔ cup [90 g] all-purpose flour

Scant ¼ tsp baking powder

4 tsp fresh thyme leaves, plus more for sprinkling

Scant ¼ tsp table salt

Scant ½ tsp cream of tartar

Confectioners' sugar for dusting

Preheat the oven to 350°F [180°C]. Line 2 baking sheets with parchment paper. Lightly grease the sides of a 9-in-by-3-in [23-cm-by-7.5-cm] springform pan with nonstick cooking spray or softened butter. Line the sides of the pan with a 3-in-by-29-in [7.5-cm-by-75-cm] strip of parchment paper.

FOR THE LADYFINGERS In the bowl of a stand mixer fitted with the whisk attachment, beat the yolks, 5 tablespoons [80 g] of the granulated sugar, and the vanilla on medium-high speed until the mixture doubles in volume and falls in a ribbon when the whisk is lifted out of the bowl, about 5 minutes.

Set a wire mesh sieve over the mixer bowl and sift the flour and baking powder into the egg mixture. Add the thyme, and very gently fold the flour mixture and thyme into the yolk mixture with a rubber spatula. The batter will be very thick. Set aside.

WHIPPED CREAM FILLING

3 cups [720 ml] heavy cream

½ cup [60 g] confectioners' sugar

3 Tbsp limoncello, optional

3 Tbsp freshly squeezed lemon juice

1 tsp lemon extract

4 cups [455 g] strawberries, sliced

In a medium bowl, add the egg whites, salt, and cream of tartar. Using an electric hand mixer, whisk on medium speed until soft peaks form. Slowly add the remaining 2 tablespoons granulated sugar. Whisk until stiff peaks form (the peaks should stand upright when the whisk is lifted from the bowl).

Using a rubber spatula, gently fold the beaten whites into the yolk mixture in three batches, until just incorporated, being careful not to decrease the volume.

Fill a pastry bag fitted with a ½-in [12-mm] round tip with batter. Pipe 3-in-by-1-in [7.5-cm-by-2.5-cm] fingers onto the two prepared baking sheets. If you do not have a pastry bag, use a large zippered plastic bag and snip off one corner. Sprinkle a couple of thyme leaves on each finger and generously sift confectioners' sugar over all of them, leaving a thick coat of sugar.

Bake one sheet at a time, rotating the pan at the halfway point, until the ladyfingers are puffy, dry to the touch, and just very slightly browned, 10 to 12 minutes. Let the ladyfingers cool in the pan for 1 to 2 minutes. Transfer them with a small offset or thin metal spatula to a wire rack to cool completely. Use immediately or freeze them on the baking sheet, then transfer to a zippered plastic bag once frozen. They will get soggy if stored in plastic on the counter. The cake can be assembled with the frozen fingers.

CONT'D

FOR THE FILLING Place the cream in the bowl of a stand mixer fitted with the whisk attachment and whisk on medium to medium-high speed until the cream begins to thicken, 2 to 3 minutes. Add the confectioners' sugar, limoncello, if using, lemon juice, and lemon extract and continue whisking until the cream holds medium peaks. Using a rubber spatula, gently fold all but a handful of the strawberries into the whipped cream.

Line the bottom and sides of the prepared springform pan with ladyfingers. Spread half of the whipped cream over the ladyfingers. Cover with another layer of ladyfingers. Repeat with the remaining whipped cream. Decorate the top with the reserved strawberries and a sprinkling of thyme leaves.

Refrigerate the cake for 24 hours, lightly covered in plastic wrap. To serve, carefully remove the sides of the pan and slice the cake using a large serrated knife. The cake will keep, lightly wrapped in plastic wrap, in the refrigerator for up to 3 days.

COCONUT-CHOCOLATE ICEBOX CAKE WITH TOASTED ALMONDS

SERVES 12

I've been dreaming about developing an icebox cake featuring the flavors of chocolate, coconut, and almond since cowriting *Icebox Cakes*. The Pecan Refrigerator Cake recipe from *Best Cake Recipes* (1929) influenced my version here. The original calls for ladyfingers layered with uncooked eggs (!) and sugar, but I chose to use chocolate wafer cookies and coconut whipped cream, made from coconut milk instead. If you have leftover whipped cream, you may use it to frost the outside of the cake, as in the picture. Although, truth be told, I prefer the cake "naked," with the layers visible for all to see.

Three 13½-fl-oz [400-ml] cans full-fat coconut milk

½ to 1 tsp almond extract

¾ cup [90 g] confectioners' sugar

1½ cups [360 ml] heavy cream

1½ cups [90 g] shredded coconut, toasted (see page 168)

9 oz [255 g] crisp chocolate wafer cookies

½ cup [60 g] sliced almonds, toasted (see page 168)

Place the cans of coconut milk in the coldest spot in your refrigerator upside-down and leave them there for 24 hours. This will allow the coconut cream in the milk to solidify and separate from the liquid.

Line a 9-by-5-by-3-in [23-by-12-by-7.5-cm] loaf pan with plastic wrap that hangs slightly over the sides of the pan.

Flip the cans of coconut milk right-side up, open the cans, and, using a rubber spatula, carefully scrape the solid coconut cream into the bowl of a stand mixer fitted with the whisk attachment. Save the liquid for another purpose. Add the almond extract and confectioners' sugar, and whisk on medium speed until smooth and thick. Add the heavy cream and whisk on medium-high speed until the cream holds stiff peaks, about 2 minutes. Add the toasted coconut and fold it into the cream with a rubber spatula.

CONT'D

Best Cake Recipes

Using a small offset spatula or the back of a spoon, spread a thin layer of the whipped cream on the bottom of the lined pan. Cover as much of the cream as possible with a layer of wafers, filling any gaps with broken wafers, to create a solid layer of wafers.

Continue layering whipped cream and wafers until you run out or reach the top of the pan, ending with a layer of wafers. Gently cover the surface with plastic wrap and refrigerate for at least 6 to 8 hours, or preferably overnight. If you have whipped cream left over, store this in the refrigerator along with the cake.

Remove the cake from the refrigerator prior to serving and peel off the plastic wrap. Place a serving plate over the pan and invert the cake onto the plate. Carefully remove the pan and plastic wrap lining and, if using, thinly spread the remaining whipped cream over the sides and top of the cake. Re-whip the cream if it looks too soft to spread. Sprinkle the cake with the toasted almonds, lightly pressing them into the cake.

Using a serrated knife, cut the cake into slices and serve. The cake will keep, lightly wrapped with plastic wrap, in the refrigerator for up to 3 days.

Note: When buying coconut milk, gently turn the can up and down in the store to make sure the contents sound full and solid. If it sounds watery and seems like the can is filled only with liquid, grab a different one.

VANILLA-RHUBARB ICEBOX CAKE

SERVES 12

I stumbled upon Fresh Rhubarb Refrigerator Cake in *250 Refrigerator Desserts* (1951). As I am a lover of both rhubarb and icebox cakes, including a version in this section of the book was a must. The original recipe calls for sweetened condensed milk, stewed rhubarb, and vanilla wafers. I've nixed the milk, substituting vanilla whipped cream in its place, for a lighter filling, and sweetened my stewed rhubarb with just a touch of sugar. I kept the vanilla wafers—they are the perfect blank canvas for the fruity filling. If rhubarb is not in season, you can substitute strawberries, fresh or frozen, in its place.

2 cups [220 g] chopped rhubarb, fresh or frozen

½ cup [100 g] granulated sugar

4 tsp pure vanilla extract

2 cups [480 ml] heavy cream

½ cup [60 g] confectioners' sugar

8 oz [230 g] vanilla wafer cookies

Red sanding sugar for decorating

Combine the rhubarb and granulated sugar in a small saucepan over medium to medium-high heat, stirring occasionally, until the fruit breaks down and is jam-like, 15 to 20 minutes. Off the heat, add 1 teaspoon of the vanilla, and set the mixture aside to cool to room temperature. The stewed rhubarb can be kept in an airtight container in the refrigerator for up to 3 days.

Have ready an 8-by-8-by-2-in [20-by-20-by-5-cm] square baking pan. Pyrex is nice, so you can see all of the layers, but not necessary.

In the bowl of a stand mixer fitted with the whisk attachment, whisk the cream on medium to medium-high speed until the cream begins to thicken, 2 to 3 minutes. Add the confectioners' sugar and the remaining 3 teaspoons vanilla, and whisk until stiff peaks form. With a rubber spatula, gently fold the room-temperature rhubarb into the cream.

Using a small offset spatula or the back of a spoon, spread a thin layer of cream on the bottom of the pan. Cover as much of the cream as possible with a layer of vanilla wafers, filling any gaps with broken wafers (breaking them yourself, if necessary). The pieces should touch. The goal is a solid layer of cookies.

Continue layering whipped cream and cookies until you run out or reach the top of the pan. Spread the top of the cake with whipped cream and gently cover it with plastic wrap. Refrigerate the cake for 6 to 8 hours, or preferably overnight.

Remove the cake from the refrigerator prior to serving and peel off the plastic wrap. Sprinkle the top of the cake with red sanding sugar.

Serve directly from the pan. The cake will keep, tightly covered with plastic wrap, in the refrigerator for up to 3 days.

MILK CHOCOLATE MALTED PUDDING

SERVES 8

No dessert quite makes me happier than chocolate pudding. I love its soft, smooth texture and pure chocolaty flavor. It can be eaten hot or cold and it's an absolute cinch to make. I came upon a chocolate malted pudding recipe in *Tested Recipes with Blue Ribbon Malt Extract* (1928). The milky, almost nutty, flavor that malt imparts when combined with chocolate is a favorite of mine, and I knew right then that my recipe would include malt as well. I substituted milk chocolate for the "square of chocolate" called for in the original. Malt's subtle flavor can get lost when combined with more bittersweet chocolate.

PUDDING

3 Tbsp Dutch-process cocoa powder

1 Tbsp granulated sugar

3 Tbsp cornstarch

⅛ tsp table salt

1½ cups [205 g] malted milk powder

2 cups [480 ml] whole milk

1 cup [240 ml] heavy cream

5 oz [140 g] milk chocolate, finely chopped

1½ tsp pure vanilla extract

CONT'D

Have ready eight ½-cup [120-ml] ramekins.

FOR THE PUDDING In a medium heatproof saucepan, add the cocoa powder, granulated sugar, cornstarch, salt, and malt powder and whisk together. Add the milk and heavy cream and whisk again.

Over medium to medium-high heat, whisk the pudding until it thickens and large bubbles begin popping up on the surface, 5 to 7 minutes. Continue whisking for 1 to 2 minutes and remove the saucepan from the heat. If it looks a bit lumpy, strain your pudding through a wire mesh sieve into a large heatproof bowl. Add the chocolate and vanilla and whisk to melt the chocolate.

CONT'D

MALTED WHIPPED CREAM

1 cup [240 ml] heavy cream

⅓ cup [45 g] malted milk powder

3 Tbsp confectioners' sugar

1 tsp pure vanilla extract

Transfer the pudding to the 8 small ramekins, cover each with plastic wrap, making sure the plastic touches the pudding to avoid a skin forming, and place in the refrigerator to set up, about 2 hours. Alternatively, keep the pudding in the large bowl, cover with plastic wrap, and place in the refrigerator to set up, about 4 hours.

FOR THE WHIPPED CREAM In the bowl of a stand mixer fitted with the whisk attachment, whisk the cream on medium to medium-high speed until the cream begins to thicken, 2 to 3 minutes. Add the malt powder, confectioners' sugar, and vanilla and continue whisking until medium peaks form.

Serve the pudding chilled, with a dollop of whipped cream on top of each ramekin.

The puddings will keep, tightly wrapped in plastic wrap, in the refrigerator for up to 3 days.

MAPLE PARFAIT WITH PECAN SANDIE CRUMBLE

SERVES 6

Recipes for maple parfait can be found in a variety of vintage booklets, which surprised me, because maple syrup is not a common ingredient in the recipes in my collection. But there's no question that maple parfait was a trendy dessert back in the day. It's almost like a maple syrup pudding, but with no thickener or additional sugar. The only ingredients are maple syrup, egg yolks, heavy cream, and finely chopped pecans. Here, I repurposed a recipe from *Auto Vacuum: Frozen Dainties* (no date), adding a bit of vanilla to the cream for a slightly more complex flavor, and some crushed pecan sandie cookies for texture.

1 cup [240 ml] maple syrup

4 egg yolks, lightly beaten

2⅓ cups [560 ml] heavy cream

1½ tsp pure vanilla extract

7 oz [200 g] whole pecan sandie cookies, crushed

1 cup [140 g] pecans, toasted and chopped (see page 168)

Set a wire mesh sieve over a small bowl. Fill a large bowl with ice. Have ready six 8-oz [240-ml] glasses.

In a small saucepan, bring the maple syrup to a boil over medium-high heat. Place the beaten yolks in a small bowl. Take the syrup off the heat, and temper the yolks by dribbling a tablespoon at a time of hot syrup into the yolks and whisking until the yolks are warm. Pour the tempered yolks into the maple syrup and whisk constantly over medium to medium-high heat until the mixture thickens and coats the back of a spoon, about 5 minutes.

Strain the mixture through the sieve into the bowl and place the bowl into the bowl of ice to cool, whisking occasionally.

CONT'D

Add the cream to the bowl of a stand mixer fitted with the whisk attachment and whisk on medium to medium-high speed until the cream begins to thicken, 2 to 3 minutes. Add the vanilla and continue whisking until soft peaks form. Pour the cooled maple mixture into the cream, and, using a rubber spatula, gently fold to combine.

Place 1 tablespoon of crushed cookies in the bottom of each of the 6 glasses. Top with the maple mixture and then again with cookies. Continue layering in this manner until full. Top with a generous tablespoon of pecans. Refrigerate for an hour before serving.

The parfaits may be stored, tightly wrapped in plastic wrap, in the refrigerator for up to 3 days.

SALTY CARAMEL CRUNCH SUNDAES WITH CARAMELIZED CORNFLAKES

MAKES 6 SUNDAES

Caramel ice cream was all the rage in the first half of the twentieth century and I discovered recipes for it in booklets dating back to the late nineteenth century. Here I've tinkered with a custard-based caramel ice cream from *Frigidaire Recipes* (1928). My recipe adds a bit of my favorite sweetener, brown sugar, to the granulated and I added twice as much vanilla and salt (to counteract the sweetness). And because I'm a sucker for any dessert that calls for cereal as an ingredient, I included caramelized cornflakes, inspired by a recipe from *Refrigerator Desserts* (1951).

CARAMEL ICE CREAM

1 cup [200 g] granulated sugar

1½ cups [360 ml] whole milk, warmed

1½ cups [360 ml] heavy cream, warmed

5 egg yolks

2 Tbsp packed light brown sugar

1 Tbsp pure vanilla extract

¾ tsp flaky sea salt

FOR THE ICE CREAM In a large deep saucepan, combine the granulated sugar and ⅓ cup [80 ml] water over high heat and cook until it boils and changes to a deep amber color, about 5 minutes. Do not stir but, holding the pan in your hands, gently swirl the mixture so the sugar cooks evenly and the color is to your liking (the deeper the color, the stronger the flavor of the caramel).

Decrease the heat to medium, and add the warm milk and cream. The mixture may bubble, so be careful. Stir the mixture with a wooden spoon until any hardened bits of caramel have melted.

In a medium bowl, add the yolks and light brown sugar and whisk until frothy and combined. Temper the yolk mixture by adding a little of the warm caramel mixture to the yolks and whisking. Continue adding the caramel to the yolks, a little at a time, until the temperature of the yolks rises. Whisking

CARAMELIZED CORNFLAKES

2 cups [55 g] cornflakes

½ cup [100 g] packed light brown sugar

2 Tbsp unsalted butter

Flaky sea salt for sprinkling

1 recipe Salty Caramel (page 114), warmed

constantly, carefully pour the tempered yolks back into the caramel, creating a custard. Stir with a wooden spoon or a heatproof spatula over medium heat until the custard thickens and your finger leaves a trail on your custard-coated spoon. Do not boil.

If lumpy, set a wire mesh sieve over a medium bowl and strain the custard into the bowl. Add the vanilla and salt and stir with a wooden spoon to combine. Place in the refrigerator, uncovered, until no longer warm, and then cover tightly with plastic wrap. Chill the custard for at least 4 hours and up to 24 hours.

Transfer the custard to your ice cream maker and freeze, following the manufacturer's instructions. Transfer to a freezer-proof container and freeze until ready to use. Homemade ice cream is best eaten within 24 hours of making.

Line a baking sheet with parchment paper.

CONT'D

FOR THE CORNFLAKES Place the cereal in a large bowl. In a small saucepan, heat the brown sugar and butter over medium-high heat until it boils. Decrease the heat to medium to medium-low and cook, stirring occasionally with a wooden spoon, for 3 to 5 minutes. The mixture may look a bit separated, but will come together as you stir. Pour the mixture over the cereal in the bowl and, working quickly, mix the cereal with the caramel using a large spoon. Transfer the mixture to the prepared baking sheet, sprinkle with flaky sea salt, and let cool. Break up big chunks with your fingers and store on the counter in an airtight container until ready to use, for up to 3 days.

To serve, place a scoop of ice cream (or two) in a bowl. Top with warmed Salty Caramel and a sprinkling of Caramelized Cornflakes.

BAKED ALASKA SANDWICH

Visually, a Baked Alaska is spectacular. Ice cream is packed into a cake-lined bowl, inverted onto a serving platter, and covered in toasted, billowy meringue. It's actually super easy to make and guests go bonkers for it. The Easy Baked Alaska from *Good Housekeeping's Cake Book* (1958) and the Baked Alaska Sandwich from *250 Refrigerator Desserts* (1951) inspired this version. I added an additional layer of cake, a variety of ice cream flavors (which looks so pretty when sliced), and was extremely generous with my meringue topping (meringue might be one of my favorite food groups). Though not technically a "sandwich," it's put together in a bread pan, making assembly and slicing the finished cake easy-peasy.

CAKE

¾ cup plus 2 Tbsp [125 g] all-purpose flour

6 Tbsp [30 g] Dutch-process cocoa powder

½ cup [100 g] packed dark brown sugar

½ cup [100 g] granulated sugar

½ tsp baking soda

Rounded ¾ tsp baking powder

½ tsp table salt

2 egg yolks

1½ tsp pure vanilla extract

¼ cup [60 ml] vegetable oil

CONT'D

Preheat the oven to 350°F [180°C]. Grease a 13-by-9-by-2-in [33-by-23-by-5-cm] pan with nonstick cooking spray or softened butter, line with parchment paper, and grease again. Line a 9-by-5-by-3-in [23-by-12-by-7.5-cm] loaf pan with a piece of plastic wrap that hangs slightly over all four sides.

FOR THE CAKE In the bowl of a stand mixer fitted with the paddle attachment, combine the flour, cocoa powder, brown sugar, granulated sugar, baking soda, baking powder, and salt on low speed until well incorporated.

In a bowl, whisk together the yolks, vanilla, oil, and buttermilk until combined. With the stand mixer on medium-low speed, slowly pour the wet mixture into the dry ingredients and beat until incorporated. Scrape down the bowl with a rubber spatula as needed.

CONT'D

½ cup [120 ml] buttermilk, at room temperature

½ cup [120 ml] boiling water

1½ tsp espresso powder

3 pt [1.4 L] ice cream, such as strawberry, chocolate, and vanilla

MERINGUE

6 egg whites, at room temperature

1 cup [200 g] granulated sugar

In the same bowl, combine the boiling water and espresso powder, add it to the batter in the mixer bowl, and mix for 30 seconds on low speed until smooth.

Pour the batter into the larger, parchment paper–lined pan and bake for 14 to 16 minutes, rotating at the halfway point. The cake is ready when a toothpick inserted in the middle comes out with a moist crumb or two. Let cool completely and freeze for 30 minutes or up to 3 days, tightly wrapped.

Place the strawberry ice cream in the microwave on high power for 20 seconds, or soften it on the counter until it scoops easily but isn't melted. Place the ice cream on the bottom of the prepared loaf pan. Drape a piece of plastic wrap over the ice cream and use your hands to press it down into a flat, even layer.

Cut the cake into three 4-in- [10-cm-] wide pieces. Place 1 piece of the cake over the strawberry ice cream and press down. Return the other 2 pieces to the freezer.

Soften the chocolate ice cream as you did the strawberry. Using plastic wrap and your hands, spread it into an even flat layer over the cake. Place another piece of the cake over the chocolate ice cream and press down. Repeat with the vanilla ice cream and the last piece of cake. The last piece will be above the edge of the pan.

Freeze until hard, at least 4 hours, preferably overnight, tightly wrapped in plastic wrap.

CONT'D

FOR THE MERINGUE Whisk the egg whites in the bowl of a stand mixer on medium-high speed until foamy. Slowly add the granulated sugar, 1 tablespoon at a time, and whisk on high speed until stiff, glossy peaks form, at least 5 minutes.

Remove the loaf pan from the freezer and lift out the cake using the plastic sling. Dip the bottom of the pan briefly in hot water if it has trouble releasing. Invert the cake onto a heatproof serving platter (the bottom layer is now the top) and generously cover the cake in meringue using an offset spatula or butter knife. Using a kitchen torch, if you have one, gently brown the meringue, or place the cake under the broiler for 1 or 2 minutes, watching closely to make sure it does not burn.

Slice the cake with a long serrated knife and serve immediately. It is best the day it is made, but will keep in the freezer, lightly wrapped in plastic wrap, for up to 3 days.

ICE CREAM CAKE

SERVES 16

The Sundae Surprise in *Let's Eat Outdoors* (1955) caught my eye right away. But instead of serving classic sundaes in little cups, I used the same classic ice cream sundae components, layered in a springform pan, starting with a graham cracker crust for texture. I topped it all with toasted walnuts and for a final touch I tossed on a few fluorescent red maraschino cherries: the perfect 1950s garnish. Be forewarned—you need to freeze each ice cream layer for an hour before adding the next, so this is a good one to make when you have time on your hands.

GRAHAM CRACKER CRUST

2 cups [240 g] graham cracker crumbs

5 Tbsp [75 g] packed light brown sugar

Rounded ¼ tsp table salt

½ cup [110 g] unsalted butter, melted

¾ tsp pure vanilla extract

3 pints [1.4 L] vanilla ice cream (or your choice)

2 cups [480 ml] Hot Fudge Sauce (page 154) or store-bought hot fudge

1 cup [240 ml] Salty Caramel (page 114) or store-bought caramel

CONT'D

Preheat the oven to 350°F [180°C]. Grease the bottom of a 9-in-by-3-in [23-cm-by-7.5-cm] springform pan with nonstick cooking spray or softened butter and line with parchment paper.

FOR THE CRUST Combine the cracker crumbs, brown sugar, and salt in the bowl of a food processer fitted with the metal blade and process until finely ground. Add the butter and vanilla and continue to process until combined. Press the mixture into the bottom of the springform pan and place in the freezer for 30 minutes.

Bake the crust for 6 to 8 minutes, rotating at the halfway point, until lightly browned and fragrant. Let the crust cool to room temperature.

CONT'D

WHIPPED CREAM

1 cup [240 ml] heavy cream

1 Tbsp confectioners' sugar

1 tsp pure vanilla extract

½ cup [60 g] walnuts, toasted, (see page 168) for decorating

Maraschino cherries for decorating

Place 1 pint [0.5 L] of ice cream in the microwave on high power for 20 seconds, or soften it on the counter until it scoops easily but isn't melted. Spread the ice cream over the graham cracker crust, cover the ice cream with a piece of plastic wrap, and use your hands to press it down into a flat, even layer. Place the pan in the freezer for at least 1 hour.

Remove the cake from the freezer, and, using an offset spatula or butter knife, spread 1 cup [240 ml] of the hot fudge sauce over the ice cream. Return to the freezer for 30 minutes. Continue layering with another layer of ice cream, the caramel, a final layer of ice cream, and a final layer of fudge, returning the cake to the freezer for about an hour after applying each ice cream layer, and 30 minutes after applying the sauces.

FOR THE WHIPPED CREAM Place the cream in the bowl of a stand mixer fitted with the whisk attachment and whisk on medium to medium-high speed until the cream begins to thicken, 2 to 3 minutes. Add the confectioners' sugar and vanilla and continue whisking until soft peaks form. Spread the whipped cream over the top layer of fudge, sprinkle with walnuts and cherries, and freeze overnight, lightly wrapped in plastic wrap. The cake can be kept in the freezer for up to 3 days before serving.

When ready to serve, remove the sides and bottom of the springform pan, using a thin spatula or paring knife to release the bottom, if necessary, and peeling off the parchment paper if it has stuck to the bottom of the cake. Let sit for 20 minutes to soften slightly.

To serve, slice with a large serrated knife dipped in very hot water. The cake will keep, tightly wrapped, in the freezer for up to 1 week.

№ **6**

Confections

"WHEN A BATCH OF CANDY IS IN THE MAKING, A FESTIVE AIR PERVADES THE KITCHEN."

— Baker's Famous Chocolate Recipes (1936)

VINTAGE ADVICE FOR THE MODERN KITCHEN

When making caramel on the stove top, cover the caramel for the first 3 minutes it boils, as the steam will melt any unwanted sugar crystallization.

HOT FUDGE SAUCE

MAKES 2 GENEROUS CUPS [480 ML]

I fell in love with hot fudge sauce at Brighams, an ice cream parlor/restaurant my dad and I used to go to on special occasions. We would sit at the counter, eating peppermint stick ice cream topped with thick, dark, oh-so-chocolaty hot fudge sauce. Here, I've tried to recreate that sauce. The recipe from *Baker's Famous Chocolate Recipes* (1936) calls for unsweetened chocolate, but I used a mix of cocoa powder and bittersweet chocolate—the combo gives the chocolate flavor of my childhood. Heavy cream gives it extra richness.

¾ cup [180 ml] heavy cream

⅓ cup [105 g] light corn syrup

5 Tbsp [75 g] granulated sugar

¼ cup [20 g] Dutch-process cocoa powder, sifted

1¼ cups [210 g] chopped 60% to 70% bittersweet chocolate

3 Tbsp unsalted butter

1 Tbsp pure vanilla extract

½ tsp table salt

In a medium saucepan, bring the cream, corn syrup, sugar, and cocoa powder to a boil over medium to medium-high heat. Add the chocolate and simmer over medium heat until the chocolate is completely melted, stirring occasionally with a wooden spoon. Take the pan off the heat and stir in the butter, vanilla, and salt.

Use immediately or transfer to a heatproof container and cool to room temperature before refrigerating. Before using, reheat the sauce by placing it in the microwave on high power for 20-second intervals, stirring after each one, until warm and pourable; or reheat in a small heatproof bowl set over a saucepan of simmering water over medium heat.

The sauce will keep for up to 2 weeks in the refrigerator, in an airtight container.

SALT-AND-PEPPER CARAMELS

MAKES 64 CARAMELS

Vintage recipes for caramels are pretty common, but it is in *Another Eighteen Unusual Recipes* (1932) that I found one featuring brown sugar. I love the molasses-like flavor that brown sugar imparts, so I used that as my base and then substituted sweetened condensed milk for the regular milk to prevent sugar crystallization and to ensure a very smooth caramel. I passed on the nuts, but I did add a generous sprinkle of flaky sea salt and freshly ground black pepper both to the hot caramel mixture as I removed it from the stove top and again directly onto the caramels as they cooled. This savory sprinkling is an unexpected, yet perfect balance to the candy's sweetness.

1½ cups [300 g] granulated sugar

½ cup [100 g] packed light brown sugar

⅔ cup [210 g] light corn syrup

1 cup [240 ml] heavy cream

½ cup [120 ml] sweetened condensed milk

5 Tbsp [75 g] unsalted butter, cubed

1 Tbsp pure vanilla extract

1 tsp flaky sea salt, plus more for sprinkling

1 tsp freshly ground black pepper, plus more for sprinkling

Grease an 8-by-8-by-2-in [20-by-20-by-5-cm] square baking pan with nonstick cooking spray or softened butter. Line with parchment paper, so that the parchment paper extends up two sides of the pan, and grease again.

In a medium deep saucepan, combine the granulated and brown sugars, ⅓ cup [80 ml] water, and corn syrup. Stir the mixture with a wooden spoon, being mindful not to splash the sides of the pan with sugar, and place the saucepan over medium-high heat. Once the mixture boils, attach a deep-fat/candy thermometer to the side of the pan, and bring the mixture to the firm ball stage, 245°F [118°C], without stirring.

CONT'D

Meanwhile, place the heavy cream, condensed milk, and butter in a small saucepan and warm this mixture on medium heat (or do so in the microwave in a microwave-safe bowl on high power). Do not let it boil or simmer, but continue to keep the mixture warm while melting the sugars.

Once the sugars reach the firm ball stage, remove the pan from the heat and add the warm cream mixture, being careful as you add it, as the caramel may splatter and bubble. Gently stir the caramel with a wooden spoon or heatproof spatula, and return it to medium heat. Continue cooking the caramel until it reaches the firm ball stage again. Do not stir. This may take a while—up to 30 minutes or longer.

Once it reaches temperature, immediately remove the caramel from the heat and add the vanilla, salt, and pepper. Stir to combine. Pour the caramel into the prepared pan, sprinkle the top with additional salt and pepper, and set aside on a wire rack until the caramel comes to room temperature, several hours.

Once cooled, lift the caramel out of the pan by the parchment paper, place it on a cutting board and, using a large knife, cut it into 1-in [2.5-cm] square pieces. Immediately wrap each piece in small squares of parchment or wax paper, twisting the ends of the paper to securely close.

The caramels will keep for up to 1 week on the counter or up to 2 weeks in the refrigerator. Bring them to room temperature before serving.

CURRIED CANDIED CASHEWS

MAKES 3 CUPS [420 G] CANDIED NUTS

As far as the perfect bar-snack goes, the sweet-salty goodness of spiced candied nuts has no equal. I was drawn to a recipe from *Candies: Made with Pet Evaporated Milk* (no date), as I like the old-school addition of evaporated milk (many candied nut recipes call for an egg white instead) and I spiced things up with curry, cayenne, and cinnamon. Cashews are used here for their deeply buttery flavor, but any nut that you like will work. These nuts keep for several weeks and make a great impromptu party snack served alongside a cheese plate with a cocktail (or two).

1 cup [200 g] packed light brown sugar

⅓ cup [80 ml] evaporated milk

1 Tbsp curry powder

1½ tsp ground cinnamon

1 tsp table salt

Rounded ¼ tsp cayenne pepper

3 cups [420 g] unsalted cashews

Flaky sea salt and freshly ground black pepper for sprinkling

Grease a baking sheet with nonstick cooking spray or softened butter and line with parchment paper. Set aside.

In a small saucepan over medium-high heat, combine the brown sugar, evaporated milk, 2 tablespoons water, curry powder, cinnamon, table salt, and cayenne. Bring to a boil and add the nuts. Cook, stirring constantly with a wooden spoon, for 8 to 12 minutes, until the nuts are thickly coated and there is little or no liquid in the bottom of the pan. Decrease the heat while stirring, if necessary, to avoid burning the nuts. Transfer the nuts to the prepared baking sheet and, as best you can, spread them in a single layer and sprinkle with sea salt and freshly ground black pepper. The mixture hardens quickly, so don't worry if the nuts end up clumping together; you can break them apart once they've cooled. Allow to dry for several hours before serving.

The nuts will keep in an airtight container on the counter for up to 3 weeks.

CINNAMON RED HOTS POPCORN

MAKES ALMOST 16 CUPS [160 G]

I am a candied popcorn fanatic and was beyond thrilled to see booklet after booklet featuring recipes for it. The candied popcorn recipe from *New Dainties Made with Domino Sugar* (1912) calls for chocolate, but I added melted cinnamon Red Hots to my popcorn instead because the combo of popcorn and the bright red candy is so pretty and surprisingly delicious (I promise). It is also extremely addictive (she writes, walking to the kitchen to grab another handful).

15 cups [135 g] popped popcorn

6 Tbsp [85 g] unsalted butter

¾ cup [150 g] granulated sugar

3 Tbsp light corn syrup

¾ cup [185 g] Red Hots or other red cinnamon candies

¾ tsp table salt

¼ tsp baking soda

Flaky sea salt for sprinkling

Preheat the oven to 250°F [120°C]. Line 2 baking sheets with parchment paper and set aside.

Place the popcorn in a large bowl. In a medium deep saucepan, stir together the butter, sugar, corn syrup, candy, ¼ cup [60 ml] water, and table salt over medium-high heat until the candy melts. Attach a deep-fat/candy thermometer to the side of the pan and boil the caramel until the temperature reaches the firm ball stage, about 245°F [118°C].

Remove the pan from the stove top, add the baking soda, and stir with a wooden spoon. Quickly pour the caramel over the popcorn and stir to thoroughly coat the popcorn in red caramel. Spread the popcorn onto the prepared baking sheets in an even layer and bake for 1 hour, rotating at the halfway point and stirring the mixture every 15 minutes.

Sprinkle with sea salt and serve in a big bowl. The popcorn is best the day it is made, but can be stored in an airtight container on the counter for up to 3 days.

PEANUT BUTTER-MARSHMALLOW KIX TREES

MAKES 16 TREES

I was instantly smitten with the Kix Cone Trees in *Betty Crocker's Good and Easy Cookbook* (1957), as they are basically a cone-shaped marshmallow Rice Krispy Treat but with Kix, a round cereal made with corn. I discovered another similar sweet in a coconut booklet, and an actual marshmallow cereal treat in *Fun with Food* by Lynne White (1957). For my version, I browned the butter (super easy to do in the microwave), and added peanut butter, vanilla, and salt. The slightly sweet cereal pairs deliciously with the nuttiness of the two butters and the vanilla and salt really help the nutty flavors pop. You can also make these in bar form and I have included instructions for doing so.

½ cup [110 g] unsalted butter

5½ cups [275 g] mini marshmallows

½ cup [130 g] creamy peanut butter (not all-natural)

6 cups [150 g] Kix cereal or other puffed corn cereal

½ tsp table salt

¾ tsp pure vanilla extract

Red and green sanding sugar for decorating

Flaky sea salt for sprinkling

Line a baking sheet with parchment paper and set aside.

To brown the butter, place the butter in a microwave-safe bowl and cover it with a microwave-safe plate. Heat on high power for 6 to 8 minutes, adding a minute or two, if necessary, until the butter has darkened and smells nutty. Combine the butter with the marshmallows and peanut butter in a large saucepan and cook over low to medium heat until melted.

Add the Kix, salt, and vanilla and mix to combine. Remove from the heat and let sit until just cool enough to handle. Then, by the (small-ish) handful, quickly begin molding the cereal into cones, placing them on the prepared sheet. Grease your hands with nonstick cooking spray if the cereal is sticking to them. Sprinkle the cones with sanding sugar and sea salt.

CONT'D

Alternatively, if you'd prefer a more traditional bar-shaped marshmallow-cereal treat, once removed from the heat, transfer the cereal-marshmallow mixture to a 13-by-9-by-2-in [33-by-23-by-5-cm] pan greased with nonstick cooking spray or softened butter, and press down with your hands or a spatula to flatten.

Sprinkle with the sanding sugar and sea salt, let come to room temperature, and cut into 16 squares. The cones (or squares) will keep on the counter, tightly covered in plastic wrap, for up to 3 days.

HONEY-ROASTED PEANUT BRITTLE

MAKES ABOUT 3½ CUPS [445 G]

Nut brittle is one of those treats with tremendous bang for the buck. It is incredibly easy to make, perfect for nibbling, and satisfies that sugar-salt craving in the snappiest of ways. Lots of booklets include brittle recipes, but it's the one from *Good Things to Eat* (1930) that I had some fun with here, boosting the flavor with honey-roasted peanuts, flaky sea salt, and vanilla. Brittle is the perfect treat for binge-watching a favorite TV show (don't ask me how I know that).

2 cups [400 g] granulated sugar

⅔ cup [210 g] light corn syrup

2½ cups [350 g] unsalted honey-roasted peanuts

2 tsp flaky sea salt, plus more for sprinkling

2 tsp baking soda

2 Tbsp unsalted butter

2 tsp pure vanilla extract

Lightly grease a baking sheet with nonstick cooking spray or softened butter. Line with parchment paper.

Combine the sugar, corn syrup, and 1 cup [240 ml] water in a medium saucepan and bring to a boil over high heat. Cook the sugar without stirring, but lift the pan off the heat and swirl its contents periodically to ensure that the sugar cooks evenly. Continue to cook until the mixture darkrens to a deep amber color, about 15 minutes (12 minutes for a golden amber, if you prefer a lighter, more sweet-tasting brittle). Remove the pan from the heat and immediately add the nuts. Stir, and add the salt, baking soda, butter, and vanilla. Stir again until incorporated.

Pour the mixture onto the prepared baking sheet and, using a small offset spatula or a butter knife greased with nonstick cooking spray or softened butter, smooth out the mixture until it is ¼ to ½ in [6 to 12 mm] thick. Sprinkle with flaky sea salt. Place the baking sheet in the freezer for 20 minutes, or on the counter for 1 hour, until the brittle has hardened.

Crack it into pieces and serve immediately or store in an airtight container on the counter for up to 3 weeks.

CHOCOLATE-MARSHMALLOW-WALNUT FUDGE WITH SEA SALT

MAKES 36 SQUARES

I rejiggered the recipe for Campfire Marshmallow Fudge from *A Book of 150 Recipes ~ Prepared with Campfire . . . Marshmallows* (1928), because I love the booklet almost as much as I love the combo of marshmallows and chocolate. To avoid using a fussy candy thermometer, I used sweetened condensed milk, which produces a fudge-like consistency in less time. Deeply toasted walnuts and a generous sprinkling of salt cut the sweetness of the marshies.

16 oz [455 g] dark chocolate, coarsely chopped

1 tsp table salt

1¼ cups [300 ml] sweetened condensed milk

1 Tbsp pure vanilla extract

2 cups [240 g] toasted walnuts (see page 168), coarsely chopped

3 cups [150 g] mini marshmallows

Flaky sea salt for sprinkling

Turbinado sugar for sprinkling

Grease an 8-by-8-by-2-in [20-by-20-by-5-cm] pan with nonstick cooking spray or softened butter. Line with parchment paper.

Put the chocolate in a large heatproof bowl and set over a saucepan of simmering water. Stir constantly with a rubber spatula until the chocolate melts. Add the salt, sweetened condensed milk, and vanilla. The chocolate may seize up temporarily. Over medium to medium-high heat, continue stirring until the mixture is smooth. Once smooth, stir for about 1 minute more, and remove from the heat.

Add the walnuts and marshmallows and stir with a wooden spoon until they are fully incorporated (the marshmallows will not melt). Transfer the fudge to the prepared pan, drape with plastic wrap, and flatten with your hands. Sprinkle with flaky sea salt and turbinado sugar.

Place in the refrigerator until hard, about 2 hours. Using a sharp paring knife, cut into 36 pieces and serve. Fudge will keep tightly wrapped on the counter for up to 1 week.

CREAM PUFFS WITH PISTACHIO PASTRY CREAM

MAKES 24 PUFFS

Cream puffs, or Party Puffs, as they are referred to in *Frozen Desserts* (no date), were a common early- to mid-twentieth-century treat, likely because they are so easy to make and yet so impressive to one's guests. Here, to the standard cream puff recipe, I added some milk along with the usual water for a softer puff. I have filled my cream puffs with pistachio pastry cream, as I love the flavor as well as its green color. I recommend serving them with a dribble of chocolate sauce. Pistachio ice cream instead of the pastry cream would be mighty tasty, too.

PISTACHIO PASTE

½ cup [70 g] shelled unsalted pistachios

2½ Tbsp granulated sugar

PASTRY CREAM

½ cup [100 g] granulated sugar

2 Tbsp cornstarch

¼ tsp table salt

1 cup [240 ml] whole milk

½ cup plus 2 Tbsp [150 ml] heavy cream

½ cup [75 g] Pistachio Paste

1 egg yolk

½ Tbsp unsalted butter

¼ to ½ tsp almond extract

Green food coloring, optional

FOR THE PASTE Add the pistachios, granulated sugar, and 1 tablespoon water to the bowl of a food processer fitted with the metal blade and pulse until a thick paste forms. Set aside.

FOR THE PASTRY CREAM In a medium saucepan whisk together the granulated sugar, cornstarch, and salt. Add the milk and heavy cream, and whisk again. Add the ½ cup [75 g] of pistachio paste and the yolk and whisk again. The paste will loosen up as it warms. Place the pan over medium-high heat and whisk the mixture until it thickens and large bubbles pop on the surface, about 5 minutes. Continue whisking for another 40 to 60 seconds, remove the pan from the heat, add the butter and almond extract, and whisk to incorporate. Add a drop of food coloring, if you desire. Transfer the pastry cream to a bowl, place plastic wrap against the surface of the cream, and refrigerate until firm, at least 2 hours. The pastry cream can be refrigerated for up to 3 days.

Preheat the oven to 425°F [220°C]. Line 2 baking sheets with parchment paper.

CREAM PUFFS

7 Tbsp [105 g]
unsalted butter

⅓ cup [65 ml] whole milk

1½ tsp granulated sugar

1 tsp table salt

1 cup [140 g]
all-purpose flour

4 eggs

EGG WASH

1 egg

Splash of heavy cream

Confectioners' sugar for
dusting

Hot Fudge Sauce
(page 154), optional

FOR THE CREAM PUFFS Add the butter, ⅔ cup [160 ml] water, milk, sugar, and salt to a medium saucepan, stirring with a wooden spoon to combine. Place over medium-high heat until the mixture just comes to a boil. Remove from the heat immediately and stir in the flour. Return the pan to medium heat and, stirring constantly, cook until the mixture thickens, becomes glossy, and begins pulling away from the bottom of the pan, about 1 minute. Transfer the dough to a bowl and stir to cool slightly, 2 to 3 minutes.

Whisk the eggs in a large measuring cup. Add to the dough a little at a time, stirring after each addition, until the dough is smooth and soft and holds together. It will appear separated, but keep stirring, adding a bit of egg, until it smoothes out. You may not need all the eggs; stop adding once the dough is glossy and thick.

Using a 1- to 1½-tablespoon cookie scoop or measuring spoon, scoop the dough onto the prepared pans, leaving about 2 in [5 cm] between scoops.

FOR THE EGG WASH Whisk together the egg and cream in a small bowl and brush the tops of the dough with the mixture. Bake for 22 to 26 minutes without opening the oven, decreasing the heat to 350°F [180°C] after 10 minutes.

Poke each puff with a toothpick to release steam. Once slightly cool, transfer to a wire rack to cool completely.

Gently cut the puffs in half with a serrated knife and fill with 1½ tablespoons of pastry cream. Dust with confectioners' sugar and drizzle with Hot Fudge Sauce, if using, and serve.

BASIC TECHNIQUES

TOASTING NUTS

Butterscotch Pecan Curls, Black-Bottom Banana Dream Bars, Peach–Graham Cracker Hazelnut Crisp, Coconut-Chocolate Icebox Cake with Toasted Almonds, Maple Parfait with Pecan Sandie Crumble, Ice Cream Cake, Chocolate-Marshmallow-Walnut Fudge with Sea Salt

Place the nuts in a single layer on a rimmed baking sheet in a 350°F [180°C] oven. Toast for 10 to 20 minutes until fragrant and lightly browned. Stir the nuts with a wooden spoon every 5 minutes or so, to ensure they brown evenly. Watch carefully—nuts can burn very quickly.

TOASTING COCONUT

Lemon Chiffon Pie with Coconut Whipped Cream,
Coconut-Chocolate Icebox Cake with Toasted Almonds

Place the coconut in a single layer on a rimmed baking sheet in a 350°F [180°C] oven. Toast for 10 to 15 minutes until fragrant and lightly browned. Stir the coconut with a wooden spoon every 5 minutes or so, to ensure it browns evenly. Watch carefully to avoid burning.

SKINNING HAZELNUTS

Peach–Graham Cracker Hazelnut Crisp

Toast the nuts and, while they are warm, rub them in a clean dish towel until the skins come off. This method does not produce perfectly skinned hazelnuts, but very close.

MAKING HAZELNUT FLOUR

Chocolate-Hazelnut Meringue Cradle Cake

Place the nuts (skinned or unskinned) in a food processer fitted with the metal blade, and process until finely ground, 2 to 3 minutes. Don't overprocess or the nuts will turn to butter.

MELTING CHOCOLATE

Cornflake Macaroons with Chocolate Drizzle,
Pumpkin-Chocolate Tart with Cinnamon Whipped Cream

Place roughly chopped chocolate in a small heatproof bowl and set over a saucepan of simmering water over medium-low heat. Make sure the bottom of the bowl is not touching the water. Stir gently with a heatproof spatula until melted. Alternatively, melt the chocolate in a microwave-safe bowl on high power in 20-second intervals, stirring the chocolate after each interval, until smooth.

BEATING EGG WHITES TO STIFF PEAKS

Silver Cake with Pink Frosting

Place the egg whites in the bowl of a stand mixer fitted with the whisk attachment, and whisk on low speed until frothy. Once frothy, gradually increase the speed to high, and whisk on high speed until they hold stiff peaks—the whites should be glossy and stand straight up when you lift the whisk, 5 to 8 minutes.

LIGHTLY SWEETENED WHIPPED CREAM

Latticed Blackberry-Lime Pie, Chocolate-Hazelnut Meringue Cradle Cake,
Cottage Pudding with Vanilla Sauce

Place the cream in the bowl of a stand mixer fitted with the whisk attachment and whisk on medium to medium-high speed until the cream begins to thicken, 2 to 3 minutes. Add about 1 tablespoon of confectioners' sugar for every 1 cup [240 ml] of cream, and 1 teaspoon of pure vanilla extract, and continue whisking until medium peaks form.

ANOTHER TOUCH OF MAGIC

ACKNOWLEDGMENTS

Thanks to Amy Treadwell, my editor, for believing in this recipe booklet–inspired cookbook, since first discussed over wine and tapas; to Judy Linden, my agent, for loving my chewy chocolate mint cookies and for always having my back (and then some). Thanks to Diana Yen, for styling, Kira Corbin, for propping, and the brilliant Alice Gao, for taking the dreamiest of photos; and to Vanessa Dina for putting said "dream(y) team" together. Thanks to Lizzie Vaughan for designing this beauty; and to Sarah Billingsley, Alexandra Brown, and Jane Horn (copy editor extraordinaire) and all the amazing peeps at Chronicle Books. It is such a pleasure and an honor to have worked with you all a second time. Thanks to EBC for too many things to name and to Bonnie Slotnick, of Bonnie Slotnick Cookbooks, for helping me build my collection of recipe booklets over the years, for advising me as I wrote this book, and for lending me many booklets from her own spectacular collection. Her shop is a great source of culinary ephemera. Thanks to Leslie M. Behm, Special Projects Librarian, Special Collections, Michigan State University Libraries, who helped me contact the companies owning the copyrights to all of the amazing vintage artwork included in this book. And thanks to Jonathan Lyons who taught me more about copyright law than I care to know. Thanks to all of the companies that generously granted me permission to use their images and to my wonderful recipe testers: Jenny A., Melissa B., Nanci B., Rebecca B., Sam C., Elaine C., Michelle C., Susan C., Urvi D., Mary Claire G., Rachel G., Jennifer H., Courtney H., Joanne H., Amy K., Amy K., Jennifer L., Molly M., Veronika M., Nefertiti M., Jenny N., Amber O., Anna P., Jess R., Helene R., Cheri R., Meg R., Janet S., Lucy S., Colleen S., Kristin S., Pom S., Wendy S., Ellen S., Caroline S., Kerstin S., Alex T., Sally T., Kim T., Mabel W., Karen W., and Stephanie W. Thanks, as always, to Matt Lewis and Renato Poliafito, for welcoming me through the bakery doors all those many eons ago, and for everything sweet that came after. And, finally, thanks to Matt, Oliver, and Jack—the three best taste testers-in-residence a girl could ask for. I love you.

BRING ON THE CRUMB JAR

BOOKLET CREDITS

11 Famous Recipes--Hershey's Cocoa. (1959). Hershey's trademarks and trade dress used with permission. For Devil's Food Sheet Cake with Sea Foam Frosting (page 97).

20 Wonderful Cakes made by the new Kraft Oil Method. (1955). Courtesy of Kraft Heinz Foods Company. For Caramel-Filled Banana Cupcakes with Penuche Frosting (page 114).

55 Recipes for Hershey's Syrup. (1945). Hershey's trademarks and trade dress used with permission. For Cornflake Macaroons (page 41).

Another Unusual 18 Recipes. (1932). The Jack Frost Sugar Logo is a Registered Trademark of Traditional Quality Corp. Used with permission. For Salt-and-Pepper Caramels (page 155).

Baker's Chocolate and Coconut Favorites. (1962). Courtesy of Kraft Heinz Foods Company. Print. For Black-Bottom Banana Dream Bars (page 61).

Best Cake Recipes. (1929). Originally published in *Better Homes and Gardens Best Cake Recipes* magazine, 1929. For Coconut-Chocolate Icebox Cake with Toasted Almonds (page 131).

Cake Secrets. (1953). Courtesy of Kraft Heinz Foods Company. For Coconut Blitz Torte (Page 110).

The Calumet Baking Book. (1931). Courtesy of Kraft Heinz Foods Company. For Swedish Tea Rolls (page 28).

The Calumet Baking Book: 89 Recipes Sure to Succeed. (1929). Courtesy of Kraft Heinz Foods Company. For Sour Cream Jumbles (page 46).

The Cookie Book. (1973). Courtesy of The Uhlmann Company. For Lemon-Pepper Shortbread (page 58).

Cookies: Westinghouse Christmas Cookie Cookbook. Courtesy of Westinghouse Electric Corporation. For Deep-Fried Cardamom Cookies (page 51).

Cookies Cookies: Made with PET Evaporated Milk. (no date). Courtesy of Eagle Family Foods Group. For Fig Pincushions (page 63).

Cookies Galore. (1956). Courtesy of Kraft Heinz Foods Company. For Peanut Butter Fingers with Salty Milk Chocolate Glaze (page 53).

Davis Master Pattern Baking Formulas. (1948). Courtesy of Clabber Girl Corporation. For Sand Tarts (page 48).

Frigidaire Recipes. (1928). Courtesy of Electrolux Home Products, Inc. For Salty Caramel Crunch Sundaes with Caramelized Cornflakes (page 142).

Frozen Desserts Made with Pet Evaporated Milk. (no date). Courtesy of Eagle Family Foods Group. For Cream Puffs with Pistachio Pasty Cream (page 166).

Fun with Food by Lynne White. (1957). Courtesy of Durkee-Mower, Inc. For Peanut Butter-Marshmallow Kix Trees (page 159).

Good Housekeeping's Book of Cookies. (1958). Courtesy of Good Housekeeping, Hearst Communications. For Butterscotch Potato Chip Balls (page 43).

Good Housekeeping's Book of Delectable Desserts. (1958). Courtesy of Good Housekeeping, Hearst Communications. For Peach-Graham Cracker Hazelnut Crisp (page 92).

Good Housekeeping's Cake Book. (1958). Courtesy of Good Housekeeping, Hearst Communications. For Baked Alaska Sandwich (page 145).

Grandma's Old Fashioned Molasses Recipes. (1928). Grandma's Molasses® is a registered trademark of B&G Foods North America, Inc. For Molasses Doughnuts with Chocolate Ginger Glaze (page 15).

Hershey's Favorite Recipes. (1937). Hershey's trademarks and trade dress used with permission. For "S'More" Graham Cracker Cake (page 120).

Home Baked Delicacies: Enhance the Fame of the Modern Hostess. Courtesy of Kraft Heinz Foods Company. For Silver Cake (page 107).

Knox Gelatin Dessert, Salads, Candies and Frozen Dishes. (1936). Courtesy of Kraft Heinz Foods Company. For Mexican Hot Chocolate Bavarian Pie (page 77).

The Latest Cake Secrets. (1934). Courtesy of Kraft Heinz Foods Company. For Lemon Chiffon Pie with Coconut Whipped Cream (page 71).

Learn to Bake: You'll Love it. (1947). Courtesy of Kraft Heinz Foods Company. For Blueberry Angel Food Dream (page 99).

The Little Book of Excellent Recipes. (no date). Courtesy of Clabber Girl Corporation. For Chai Banana Fritters (page 18).

Metropolitan Cook Book. (1933). Courtesy of MetLife Archives. For Cacio e Pepe Popovers (page 33).

My Party Book of Tested Chocolate Recipes. (1938). Courtesy of Kraft Heinz Foods Company. For Chocolate Peppermint Stick Roll (page 104).

Secrets of the Jam Cupboard. (1930). Courtesy of Kraft Heinz Foods Company. For Strawberry-Basil Turnovers (page 89).

Some of My Favorite Good Things to Eat. (1940). © Church & Dwight Co., Inc. Use of ARM & HAMMER recipe booklet images is with the express written permission of Church & Dwight Co., Inc., Ewing Township, New Jersey. For Strawberry Shortcake (page 122).

Successful Baking for Flavor and Texture. (1940). Courtesy of Kraft Heinz Foods Company. For Vanilla Yogurt Coffee Cake (page 30).

Tested Recipes with Blue Ribbon Malt Extract. (1928). Courtesy of Premiere Malt Products, Inc. For Milk Chocolate Malted Pudding (page 136).

INDEX